Fred H. Fechel

RELIGION, SCIENCE, AND MENTAL HEALTH

Proceedings of the First Academy Symposium on Inter-discipline Responsibility for Mental Health — a Religious and Scientific Concern • 1957

ACADEMY OF RELIGION AND MENTAL HEALTH

with the aid of

THE JOSIAH MACY, JR. FOUNDATION

NEW YORK
UNIVERSITY
PRESS • 1959

COMMITTEE ON ARRANGEMENTS

Harvey J. Tompkins, M.D., *Chairman*

The Rev. George C. Anderson

The Rev. William C. Bier, S.J., PH.D.

Frank Fremont-Smith, M.D.

The Rev. Hans Hofmann, PH.D.

Rabbi I. Fred Hollander

Lawrence C. Kolb, M.D.

Earl A. Loomis, Jr., M.D.

The Rev. Kenneth W. Mann, PH.D.

The Rev. Otis Rice, D.D.

PREFACE

The proceedings presented in this volume comprise the substance of a three-day conference held December 6th–8th, 1957, at Arden House, Harriman, New York. This conference represented the first Academy Symposium of a relatively new organization: the Academy of Religion and Mental Health. Proper appreciation of the conference and of its proceedings is dependent upon a knowledge of the nature of the Academy (which is unique) and of its purposes (which are multiple). Hence a preparatory historical note about the Academy will first be offered.

The Academy represents the response of one group of people to the urgency and magnitude of the mental health problem. Mental and emotional illness, as statistics only too clearly demonstrate, constitute the greatest health problem in our country today. The dimensions of the task in this area are formidable, and require the use of all the resources at our disposal. One of the principal inspirations for the formation of the Academy has been the recognition that the two greatest healing powers known to man—medicine and religion—have insufficiently collaborated in the area of mental health, and it was largely to foster such collaboration that the Academy was founded.

The medical specialty concerned with mental illness is, of course, psychiatry, and even the most passing acquaintance with the history of this specialty is sufficient to reveal the strained relationship that existed from the beginning between psychiatry and religion. There were extremists who contributed to this estrangement from both sides: psychiatrists who saw religion as an obstacle to mental health, and clergymen who saw psychiatry only as an enemy of religion. Calmer voices have now come to prevail in both camps.

Psychiatry today is willing to acknowledge that mental health extends beyond preventive psychiatry, and that the battle with mental illness is to be won only with the aid of many allies. One such powerful ally, whose potential in this area has scarcely been tapped, is religion, and psychiatry has gradually come to accept and, indeed, to seek the help to be secured from this source. Admittedly, this is a change of attitude, if not for all psychiatrists, at least for the profession as a whole.

The late R. Finley Gayle, M.D., was speaking for the profession in his presidential address, delivered at the 1956 meeting of the American Psychiatric Association, to which he gave the title: *Conflict and Co-operation between Psychiatry and Religion.* In his talk Dr. Gayle declared that the conflict between psychiatry and religion had "subsided remarkably within the past few years," so that he was inclined to characterize the present status as one of "peaceful co-existence," and encouraged to call for a gradual moving into a period of "active co-operation." Effective co-operation would become possible, Dr. Gayle thought, with "properly qualified persons in both professions working closely together."

The movement toward the acceptance of religion as a professional ally on the part of psychiatry has been matched by a similar trend toward psychiatry on the part of clergymen. The suspicion of psychiatry that almost universally characterized an earlier generation of clergymen has been gradually giving way in our own time to an appreciation of the help that religion can secure from psychiatry, and the actual need of the latter for certain types of parishioners.

Within each of the major religious groups there are significant indications of a growing acceptance of psychiatry. Publications such as *Pastoral Care* and *Pastoral Psychology* among Protes-

The conference ran from a Friday afternoon to a Sunday noon, December 6th to 8th, 1957. The initial gathering on Friday afternoon was given over to matters of organization, the introduction of conference members to one another, and such preliminary concerns. The first regular session of the symposium on Friday evening was devoted to the behavioral sciences, as represented by two psychologists, O. Hobart Mowrer, PH.D., and Abraham Maslow, PH.D. The medical men had their say on Saturday morning in the persons of Harold G. Wolff, M.D., and Gregory Zilboorg, M.D., while on Saturday afternoon the clergymen took the floor. In this session, the Rev. Hans Hofmann, PH.D., the Rev. Noël Mailloux, O.P., and Rabbi Albert A. Goldman presented the viewpoints of their own faiths. Saturday evening was reserved for informal discussions in impromptu groups on matters growing out of or allied to the materials of the three formal sessions of the symposium. The concluding session on Sunday morning was devoted to a distillation of the preceding sessions and a focusing on the problems that emerged, with a view to future work.

The main purpose of the symposium was to bring together for three days of mutual confrontation and discussion representatives of the three major fields already alluded to in a multi-faceted and multi-discipline approach to mental health. It was desired to create an atmosphere in which perfectly frank and spontaneous conversations could take place. Consequently, no representatives of the press were invited lest the prospect of publicity hamper freedom of expression. A full transcript was made of the three major sessions, for the private use of the participants and to facilitate the task of the editorial committee in preparing the present volume of published proceedings.

Though a free interplay of discussion was sought, it was realized in planning the conference that some antecedent preparation and structuring was necessary, to provide a springboard for the discussion and to prevent certain salient points from being omitted from consideration. Consequently the persons mentioned above were invited, prior to the conference, to prepare statements reflecting their views, as representative people in their respective fields, on the bearing of their specialty on mental health. In order that these formal presentations might not dwarf the main work of the discussion, they were sharply limited in time, and the role of *initiating* discussion was impressed upon the speakers.

Each of the persons who gave a formal presentation equivalently said to his colleagues in his own specialty and to the members of the other disciplines gathered for the conference: "Here are my views, or at least some of them, on mental health. What is your reaction to them?" The discussions provoked in this way turned up some encouraging areas of agreement, a number of which cut sharply across specialty lines, some disagreements (and sometimes an insight into the reasons for them), and many areas for future work and exploration.

Desirable as was the emphasis on spontaneity for the conference itself, transferring that quality to the printed page presented problems to the editorial committee. Discussions that seem so lively and pertinent when they take place lose much of their flavor and pointedness in the transcription. It is even possible to draw from a written account a rather different impression from one gathered at the conference table. Another obvious problem stems from the fact that not all verbalizations are equally valuable and therefore equally worthy of publication. What satisfies very well as a spontaneous remark in a spirited discussion may not be equally suitable for inclusion in a permanent record. It was clear that a considerable amount of editorial work and discretion would be involved in readying the discussions for publication.

Faced with these problems, the editorial committee made two basic decisions, one with respect to the formal papers, the other with reference to the discussions. Since the formal papers furnished the point of departure and the basis for subsequent discussions, the latter would have lacked a setting and to a considerable extent even a meaning without the presentation of the antecedent papers. Consequently the committee decided to publish each of the formal papers presented at the symposium. With respect to the discussions, the committee determined that they would emphasize the thread and trend of *ideas* rather than the contributions of individual conference members. In this way it was felt that the work of the conference, both with respect to the ideas presented and the problems encountered, could more clearly and more readily be presented. This decision meant, of course, that the committee assumed the responsibility for select-

TABLE OF CONTENTS

RELIGION, SCIENCE, AND MENTAL HEALTH

ing, emphasizing, and formulating the ideas found in the discussions as presented in this volume. The proceedings thus represent the pooled thinking of the conference as filtered through the editorial committee rather than the specific contributions of individual members.

The formal papers as they appear in the following pages are the result of a revision of their original remarks on the part of each of the authors. The revision has resulted in a lengthening of the papers in certain instances. The expansion has been made at the suggestion of the editorial committee in cases where clarification of the author's position was brought out in the subsequent discussion. The points thus clarified logically belong with the initial presentation, and they were incorporated into it in the revision.

The chapters in this volume follow the general structure of the symposium. A chapter is given to each of the three major approaches to mental health represented in the Academy and considered in the conference, namely, the behavioral sciences, medicine, and religion. Another chapter reports the Sunday morning session, which, in addition to summarizing the conference itself, considered problems of future work and study in the area of mental health. This chapter bears the significant title: *Horizons for the Future*. The final chapter is an evaluation and a valedictory.

A grant from the Josiah Macy, Jr. Foundation made possible both the convoking of the conference and the publication of the proceedings. To this foundation and to its medical director, Frank Fremont-Smith, M.D., the editorial committee, in the name of the Academy of Religion and Mental Health, wishes to express its deep gratitude. Thanks are also expressed to the members of the conference who generously gave time and thought—two priceless commodities—to the work and the success of the conference.

The Academy symposium reported in this volume is not thought of as an isolated conference, but rather as one of a series of which the present conference is simply the first. The Josiah Macy, Jr. Foundation has already assured the Academy of a grant that will make possible the continuance of the conference for 1958. Such a continuing study of mental health on the part of the disciplines represented is thought to involve not only a series of annual conferences, but to include study groups on specific topics, operating during the year between the conferences.

In the annual conferences it is conceived that there will be a sufficient core of the same people to insure continuity, and enough turnover of conference members to guarantee diversity and freshness of viewpoint. To the reader of this report, and especially of the final chapter, it will be abundantly clear that ground has indeed been broken by the present conference in terms of a multi-discipline approach to mental health, but that much more work remains to be done.

THE EDITORIAL COMMITTEE:

Harvey J. Tompkins, M.D., *Chairman*
The Rev. George C. Anderson
The Rev. William C. Bier, S.J., PH.D.
John Melton Cotton, M.D.
Rabbi I. Fred Hollander
Earl A. Loomis, Jr., M.D.
The Rev. Noël Mailloux, O.P.

tants, both of which endeavor to bring psychological and psychiatric insights to bear upon the work of the ministry; the increasing number of Pastoral Psychology Institutes for the Clergy conducted under Catholic auspices or with Catholic approval and support; and the Institute of Pastoral Psychiatry established in connection with the New York Board of Rabbis—all are diversified instances of a widespread willingness on the part of the clergy to assimilate and utilize the findings of psychiatry.

Discerning these significant movements within the psychiatric and the religious fields, several Protestant clergymen at St. Luke's Hospital, New York City, thought that the time was ripe in 1953 for the launching of an organization that would serve to bring together representatives from these two, as well as other related disciplines. The vehicle that grew out of their deliberations was the National Academy of Religion and Mental Health, formally created as a nonprofit organization in July, 1954, under a petition granted by the Common Pleas Court of Delaware County, Pennsylvania. There intervened a period of two years devoted to earnest, private conversations with representatives of religion, psychiatry, and allied fields. These soundings were eminently fruitful, not alone in the encouragement received, but in the readiness of able and distinguished men to volunteer their time and talents as members of the Advisory Council.

Within the bare three years since the public announcement of the founding of the Academy, it has secured some 3,000 members among individuals and institutions. In recognition of its expanding work and services, which are no longer limited to this country, the word National has been deleted from the name of the Academy. The prime mover in all this work has been the Reverend George Christian Anderson, an Episcopal clergyman and formerly a chaplain at St. Luke's Hospital, who was the principal founder and organizer of the Academy and who became its first director.

Dedicated to an inter-discipline approach to mental health, the Academy sought to interest in the undertaking, not only the two basic groups of medicine and religion already mentioned, but allied disciplines as well. Thus from the beginning, representatives of the behavioral sciences were brought into the Academy, especially psychologists and social workers to whom mental health was an obvious professional concern. There are other members not professionally connected with the medical or behavioral sciences or the clergy, but whose interest in human well-being prompts them to ally themselves with the Academy's undertakings.

The Academy has devoted itself to a program of education and action in the area of mental health. Despite its youth, it can point to several noteworthy accomplishments. Chief, perhaps, among these is the five-year pilot and evaluation study, currently under way at Harvard, Loyola (Chicago), and Yeshiva universities, designed to develop mental health curricula that may be incorporated into the theological schools of the country and thus afford a supply of clergymen better qualified to understand the emotional problems of the people to whom they will minister. The Academy served to initiate the discussions leading to the development of these three parallel programs; helped to secure from the National Institute of Mental Health the grant that makes those possible; and has from the outset served as consultant on the project to the universities concerned. Also worthy of mention is the work of the Academy in securing a grant (since repeated) from the Smith, Kline & French Foundation to finance fellowships for theological students and clergymen desirous of securing special training to qualify themselves as mental hospital chaplains. A third accomplishment was the preparation and publication of a 112-page *Manual of Procedures, Topics and Materials for Discussions in Mental Health,* now in use among educational, professional, and community groups throughout the country.

The symposium presented in this volume is the first national-level conference sponsored by the Academy and conducted with the over-all purpose of exploring the bearing of religion, medicine, and the behavioral sciences upon mental health. True to its own multi-discipline orientation, the initial academy symposium of the Academy took as its title: *Inter-discipline Responsibility for Mental Health—A Religious and Scientific Concern.*

The persons invited to attend the symposium represented the three major groups that the Academy was designed to bring together, namely: medical men, clergymen, and behavioral scientists. Apart from an introductory and a concluding meeting, the conference consisted of three main sessions, each devoted to a consideration of one of these three approaches to mental health.

RELIGION, SCIENCE, AND MENTAL HEALTH

to reach agreement among themselves, Dr. Fremont-Smith remarked. They run into the same communication problems that plague all branches of science when their representatives come together. Similar difficulties in understanding each other have traditionally existed among the several religious faiths. Problems of this kind would certainly arise in this gathering, he said. Bringing together behavioral scientists with their communication difficulties and religionists with theirs would produce still another set of difficulties between the two groups. A special goal of the conference was to try to overcome these problems.

"It has been the tradition of both groups to give lectures," Dr. Fremont-Smith continued. "A lecture has an overt purpose—to convey a message; but it has also a hidden motivation: for the lecturer to hear his own words delivered by his own voice for his own satisfaction." In a conversation, however, the other person is there, with interruptions and nonverbal signals, changes in facial expression, nods and smiles, or indications of dissent. The lecturer may be totally unaware of the reaction of his listeners; in a conversation, each person is conscious of the response of his *vis-à-vis*. The conference Dr. Fremont-Smith regarded as the most rewarding technique because it combines the advantages of the lecture—an opportunity for a participant to air his views at some length—with the opportunities afforded by conversation for interruption, expression of agreement or disagreement, and—especially important—for clarification of one's thoughts by hearing himself express them. "How do I know what I think until I hear what I say?" Also, many thoughts are undoubtedly called into being by the expression of another person's ideas.

Continuity of a conference program is most important, Dr. Fremont-Smith said. He had observed from conference-program experience that succeeding conferences do not start at the full point reached at the end of the preceding one, but about halfway along the line. They move along quickly to the end point of the former gathering and then reach into new territory, so that progress becomes more noticeable with each new meeting of the group.

Dr. Appel closed the orientation session with announcements and verification of assignments.

CONTRIBUTIONS AND RESPONSIBILITIES OF THE

BEHAVIORAL SCIENCES WITH SPECIAL EMPHASIS

ON PSYCHOLOGY, SOCIOLOGY, AND

CULTURAL ANTHROPOLOGY

CHAIRMAN
Otto Klineberg, M.D., PH.D.

DISCUSSION LEADERS
O. Hobart Mowrer, PH.D.
Abraham Maslow, PH.D.

CONTRIBUTIONS AND RESPONSIBILITIES OF THE

BEHAVIORAL SCIENCES WITH SPECIAL EMPHASIS

ON PSYCHOLOGY, SOCIOLOGY, AND

CULTURAL ANTHROPOLOGY

INTRODUCTION BY CHAIRMAN KLINEBERG

This evening we are to look at the relations between certain aspects of the behavioral or social sciences, particularly the relations between psychology and religion. The topic is one of long-standing interest to psychologists. We are all familiar with the classical book by William James, *Varieties of Religious Experience*.[1] Since then, psychologists have written many books in an attempt to understand religious behavior and to see the interrelationship

---

[1] James, William, *Varieties of Religious Experience*. Longmans, Green & Co., New York, 1925.

between psychological theory and research on the one hand and religious experience on the other. One of the most recent is *The Individual and His Religion*,[2] from the pen of a man whom many of us know and greatly admire, Gordon W. Allport, of Harvard.

It is a pleasure, indeed, to preside at a meeting in which the discussion will be opened by two old friends and colleagues. I don't see them often enough, but I know that from Hobart Mowrer and Abraham Maslow we will get a very good start in the discussion and in raising some of these issues.

Since our agenda is flexible, I have decided to call on them in reverse alphabetical order, and I now suggest to Dr. Hobart Mowrer that he take the stand.

PRESENTATION BY DR. MOWRER

Coming out here from Chicago on the train last night I opened a book that I had been looking forward to reading. The first two sentences of the preface had, it seemed to me, a peculiar bearing on this conference. The book is Kenneth Boulding's new one called *The Image*,[3] which I commend to you for many reasons, and the sentences I mentioned are these:

This book is the result of the impact of a unique experience and a unique institution. I spent the academic year 1954–55 at the Center for Advanced Study in the Behavioral Sciences at Stanford, California, described by a perceptive Catholic priest as 'a retreat house for the intellect.'

I think all of us have a little bit the feeling that we have come, at least for a weekend, to a kind of retreat house where there can be reflection and communication with people in other but related and sympathetic fields. Speaking as a representative of the behavorial sciences, I want to say that this is a privilege, and we are very grateful to the people who have made this pleasant occasion possible.

Dr. Maslow and I have been asked to open the discussion this evening on the contributions and responsibilities of the behavorial sciences to the field of religion and mental health, with

2 Allport, Gordon W., *The Individual and His Religion*. The Macmillan Co., New York, 1950.

3 Boulding, Kenneth E., *The Image*. University of Michigan Press, Ann Arbor, Mich., 1956.

special emphasis on psychology, sociology, and anthropology. I thought of several possible ways of trying to do this, but the one that seemed best to me involves an effort to view our task in a broad historical and cultural perspective.

Many of you will recall that in his *General Introduction to Psychoanalysis*,[4] Freud singled out three major developments in science that, as he put it, "have disturbed the sleep of the world." By this last it was apparent that he was referring to the settled, more or less comfortable and unified beliefs of established religion, traditional religion.

The first of these scientific discoveries, or theories, to which Freud alluded was advanced by Copernicus, who held that the earth was not the center of the universe as previously believed. As we know, this view—now generally accepted—had a very unsettling effect, intellectually and emotionally, for a considerable time.

The second of these disturbing developments was the Darwinian theory that man is a product of organic evolution instead of being especially created, as orthodox religion maintained.

And, as you can well imagine, Freud held that the third of these developments that had disturbed the sleep of the world was psychoanalysis itself, with its emphasis on complete psychic determinism and the notion of unconscious motivation.

Now, I think we have to admit that by the end of the nineteenth century religion was in an awkward position and decidedly on the defensive. It had long since lost the battle with Copernicus, and its defeat on the score of evolution now also seemed assured. With the advent of psychoanalysis and the emergence of the behavioral sciences in general, many persons, both inside and outside the Church, were prepared for a third blow that might prove the most devastating of all. Freud himself, of course, was frank to say that he regarded religion as infantile nonsense, and that he hoped soon to see mankind rid of it.[5]

It seems to me that one of the first things we ought to do is to ask ourselves to what extent the expected developments in psychology, psychoanalysis, and the related sciences have actually materialized. There was a period when it looked as if the de-

---

[4] Freud, S., *A General Introduction to Psychoanalysis*. Liveright Publishing Corp., New York, 1920.

[5] Freud, S., *The Future of an Illusion*. Hogarth Press, London, 1928.

Psychology, Sociology, and Cultural Anthropology

velopment of psychoanalysis and the related sciences was going to bring about the final demise of organized religion. That, of course, has not come about. But I think we can say, very definitely, that two things have happened. How much of a margin of safety remained I don't know; but for a considerable time organized religion found itself in a badly discredited and weakened state and almost capitulated. Theologians were turning to psychoanalysis rather than to their own great traditions for guidance. Many people in high places were saying that all ministers ought to be psychoanalyzed.

Following that, and almost miraculously it seems, there has been a recovery, a very remarkable recovery, of religion in this country and to some extent on a world-wide scale. In 1936 the psychologist H. C. Link wrote a prophetic little book called *The Return to Religion.*[6] Most of his contemporaries thought that he didn't know what he was talking about; but he foresaw some of the blind alleys that we were moving into when he wrote this very fine and modern little book. Will Herberg, in a book called *Protestant, Catholic, and Jew,*[7] has recently documented *The Return to Religion* from a sociological point of view; and the statistics that he provides confirm on a national scale the things that we have all seen in our local communities and on our campuses.

The amount of intellectual ferment in the theological and religious fields today is very striking. I feel that some of the most stimulating and worth-while books now being published today fall in this general area. Periodicals have been established, and the emergence of organizations such as this Academy provide further testimony of this development. Religion is definitely not dead, and it seems presently to have great new vitality and promise.

So I think we can say, then, that these two things are clear. One is that religion came near eclipse; the second is that it made a remarkable recovery. What is not so clear is the nature of the impact all this is having and will continue to have for some time to come upon the so-called behavioral sciences. For a while, they thought that they were about to "take over," if I may use that term. Well, they have not; and as I see it, this has produced a

6 Link, H. C., *The Return to Religion*. The Macmillan Co., New York, 1936.
7 Herberg, W., *Protestant, Catholic, and Jew*. Doubleday & Co., Garden City, N. Y., 1956.

crisis in the behavioral sciences, the impact and implications of which have yet to be fully discerned and appraised.

Whatever the answer may be to this question of what is happening to the behavioral sciences, I would say that those of us who here represent these areas must approach our task with diffidence and caution. It is almost presumptuous at this stage for us to speak about the "contributions" of the behavioral sciences. During this period of crisis and self-examination, when we are not in the strong position we fancied ourselves to be in some ten or twenty years ago, we can hardly step forward and tell theologians and the rest of the world what is what.

With these preliminary considerations in mind, I suggest that we turn to the rather tentative propositions that have been mimeographed and distributed to you earlier this afternoon. These are put forward not as questions, but as declarative sentences because I felt that I could communicate perhaps more effectively in this way. I hope you will regard them all as questions and questionable.

The first proposition is: *The behavioral sciences are currently in crisis and are being influenced more by religion than the other way round.* My preceding remarks elaborate on that somewhat, and perhaps we should pass on to the next one.

The second proposition is: *Experimental psychology is only now taking cognizance of problems with which religion has long been concerned.* Here I want to take just a moment to trace briefly the recent history of experimental psychology. Prior to the turn of the century, psychology was largely structuralism, and its principal method was that of introspection. Psychologists were interested in consciousness and total experience; but they had very poor methods, and they were making no progress in comparison with physiology and related sciences. So there was a kind of revolution, and all of this was thrown out. The cry of the day was, "Let us get back to observable data exclusively, to stimulus and response." Even the organism was thrown out. The abstraction was just stimulus and response; and, of course, this led to so-called radical behaviorism.

Toward the end of the second decade of this century, Robert Woodworth said, "Isn't this a little too much of an abstraction? Isn't there, really, when you come to think of it, an organism in between the stimulus and the response?" And he went on to ask,

"Couldn't we change our formula to S-O-R instead of S-R? We will admit there is nothing much in the organism. We are in the era of the empty organism, essentially, but let us just pay homage to its presence at any rate."

In the last three decades or so a very interesting thing has been going on. Little by little we have been filling that organism up again. Tolman came along with his concept of intervening variables. One of these, discovered some fifteen years ago, was fear and relief from fear. We had to have that in order to make our system work. Also, within the last fifteen years or so, we have discovered something that we call secondary motivation. If you translate that expression into English, it turns out to be *hope*; and when a hope is not fulfilled, then you have disappointment—frustration.

Some experimental psychologists have even begun investigating the phenomenon of courage in rats; and they may eventually get around to conceptualizing and having a methodology for the study of guilt. But you see how extremely primitive these concepts and levels of exploration are.

The system that experimental psychology, as behaviorism, has developed is extremely simple, primitive, and incomplete; and despite the fact that I am working on a book in this area, I must say that I don't think it contributes a thing, really, to the issues of more ultimate concern that bring us together here. I would be very glad to be challenged on this score; but my considered opinion is that behavioristic psychology doesn't have anything authoritative to say in the areas of religion and mental health at present. As a friend of mine puts it: "It is still in the process of catching up with common sense."

The third proposition is: *Clinical psychology is in transition from a former emphasis on repression and release of repression to the concepts of alienation and reconciliation.* Alienation actually is a very old psychiatric term; but it appears that it is a very good one and, interestingly enough, it is coming back into vogue. There are many things that could be said by way of documenting this; and I have a number of excerpts with me from a book called *Progress in Psychotherapy* [8] edited by Frieda Fromm-Reichmann and J. L. Moreno, to which Dr. Zilboorg and perhaps

[8] Fromm-Reichmann, Frieda, and Moreno, J. L., editors, *Progress in Psychotherapy*. Grune & Stratton, New York, 1957.

others of you have contributed. We can turn in that particular direction, if you wish.

The fourth proposition, a statement made by one of the contributors to the volume I have just mentioned, is: *Reductionism ("Man is nothing but . . .") has reached an impasse, and there is active reconsideration of the nature of man.* This view is cropping up in all kinds of unexpected places. For example, the National Academy of Psychotherapists had a meeting in New York in 1957, nominally on different value systems. I did not attend, but I heard tape recordings of the speeches, and they all dealt with different conceptions of the nature of man. This is typical of the growing interest in such issues.

Gordon Allport, if he were here, could speak to us about writing he has done in the last fifteen or twenty years about the use of models—the machine model, the infant model, the animal model, and so on—in psychology,[9] which are not iconic, as Charles Morris [10] would say, with the subject. They are not adequate to the subject that we are interested in, namely man, and apparently we cannot conceptualize man successfully on the basis of any of these incomplete models.

A couple of weeks ago I attended a meeting of the Religious Education Association in Chicago. The entire program was on the images of man, which shows that this is very much in the air and under debate at the present time. One of the reasons why existentialism has made such inroads on psychiatry, psychology, and religion, is that we had completely ignored many of the existential issues that are uniquely human. At the meeting I just mentioned, somebody defined man as *the animal that knows he is going to die.* Here is an implication for human existence that we have very largely ignored in the behavioral sciences and that the existentialists have been bringing to our attention.

The fifth proposition is: *The notion of the unconscious is being re-examined and re-evaluated.* Freud's premise that neurosis arises from repressed impulses swept the field, of course. It underwent some revision at the hands of such men as Wilhelm

---

9 Allport, Gordon W., "Scientific Models and Human Morals." *Psychological Review*, 1947, *54*, 182–192.

10 Morris, C., *Signs, Language, and Behavior.* Prentice-Hall, Inc., New York, 1946.

Psychology, Sociology, and Cultural Anthropology

Stekel [11] and Anton Boisen.[12] The notion was then explored that it is not *id* or impulse or instinct that is repressed and needs to be released, perhaps, so much as it is *superego*. This idea has much validity, I think, but it still isn't the whole story. If time permits, I would like to invite your attention to what I regard as the Old Testament conception of psychopathology. It presents a very different and perhaps much more valid conception of psychopathology than we find in either of these notions of repression that I have just mentioned.

The sixth proposition is: *There is widespread disagreement and uncertainty about the nature of psychotherapy.* A few months ago two psychologists in Chicago who have collected a set of documents that they call *Critical Incidents in Psychotherapy* sent them around to a number of people for comment and discussion. Here I was amazed to find the utter lack of anything that might pass as orthodoxy or agreement in the field of psychotherapy. Orthodoxy is apparently in a state of collapse in this field. There is a lot of intelligent experimentation going on; but we cannot say nay to anything at present because of the great variety of things that are being done in the name of psychotherapy. I have these documents with me, and if you want to go further into this area we can explore that, too. I would like to add a comment that appears in Dr. Zilboorg's chapter in the book I referred to earlier, *Progress in Psychotherapy.* He says: "Psychotherapy is today in a state of disarray almost exactly as it was two hundred years ago," and being not only a psychoanalyst and a psychiatrist but a medical historian as well, he is in a position to make such a statement.

The seventh proposition is: *Research is always useful, but often in but limited ways.* I think we have overevaluated the importance and the scope, the *possible* scope, of research in the behavioral sciences, because some of the problems in this area are of such magnitude that you cannot test them with nonsense syllables, you cannot test them even with group dynamics. Nothing smaller than the total sweep of history will provide the test for some issues and problems. This ought to counsel considerable humility in our estimate of the extent to which research in this

[11] Stekel, Wm., *Technique of Analytical Psychotherapy.* Liveright Publishing Corp., New York, 1950.
[12] Boisen, A. T., *The Exploration of the Inner World.* Harper & Bros., New York, 1936.

area, in the conventional sense of the term, is going to give us the answers.

Finally, and not because it exhausts the possible topics but simply because I didn't want to list too many here, is this proposition: *The practices of so-called primitive peoples are often instructive and raise grave questions concerning some of our own attitudes and actions in the area of mental health.*

I am not going to try to elaborate on this last point except to say that some of us, coming out in the bus this afternoon, and again at dinner, were talking about it and related considerations. We could have a lively discussion on this proposition if you care to pursue it.

Some months prior to the conference, Dr. Mowrer was asked to submit a series of propositions as a basis for discussion. The following were submitted:

1. The behavioral sciences are currently in crisis and are being influenced more by religion than the other way round.

2. Experimental psychology is only now taking cognizance of problems with which religion has long been concerned.

3. Clinical psychology is in transition from a former emphasis on repression and release to the concepts of alienation and relationship.

4. Reductionism ("Man is nothing but . . .") has reached an impasse, and there is active reconsideration of the nature of man.

5. The notion of the "unconscious" is being re-examined and re-evaluated.

6. There is widespread disagreement and uncertainty about the nature of psychotherapy.

7. Research is always useful but often in limited ways; some problems are too large for research in the ordinary sense and history becomes our only laboratory.

8. The practices of so-called primitive peoples are often instructive and raise grave questions concerning some of our own attitudes and actions in the area of mental health.

COMMENTS BY CHAIRMAN KLINEBERG

Dr. Mowrer gave us a number of possibly controversial issues. Here are some I noted that you may keep in mind for discussion.

He spoke of the relation between Freud's writing and religion, saying that he believed Freud personally was antireligious, and that psychoanalysis had been influenced by Freud's attitude toward religion.

Dr. Mowrer offered the interesting proposition that religion almost went under following the growth of psychoanalysis and in the face of general scientific advances. At least it was severely damaged as a significant, established factor in men's lives by the end of the nineteenth century. It has in recent decades, however, made a strong recovery. I should like to ask why the return to life, a question that may be answered somewhat differently by the psychologists, the psychiatrists, and the religious leaders.

Dr. Mowrer said also that the recovery of religion has had and will continue to have a strong influence on the behavioral sciences. I should like to see the effect of religion and the posing of religious questions upon the behavioral sciences discussed, and the extent to which the direction of interest and research in psychology has been influenced by religion.

With Dr. Mowrer's remarks upon the limitations of experimental psychology in mind, may we consider just how much it has to offer? What can research do? Exactly what are its limitations?

Another highly interesting point is: what can we learn from other cultures?

PRESENTATION BY DR. MASLOW

I think I will use my ten minutes best by filling in some of the background of research and exploration that led me to make these propositions you have before you, and others that I could have added.

I feel much more optimistic than Dr. Mowrer does about the possibilities of research in these areas. If only he would permit me to define research much more broadly, more in the way in which it was defined about three or four hundred years ago, I think research very definitely is possible on the questions that concern us, and I have tried to do some myself.

One simple-minded, obvious kind of thing that I started to do about fifteen years ago was simply to select the good men, admirable human beings, whom later on I got to call "healthy human beings," although it didn't start that way, and simply to observe them, to question them, to question the people who knew them, and to introspect on my own relations with them, to try to understand what are the descriptive characteristics of the human beings whom we actually call our best human beings.[1]

---

[1] Maslow, A. H., *Motivation and Personality*. Harper & Bros., New York, 1954.

all on the same few pages it then becomes quite clear that Freud, for instance, has advanced not just one theory, but many contradictory ones. He didn't have a single theory of love at all. On the whole, it is missing from the psychoanalytic system. Where he does comment or formulate a theoretical statement on love, it is contradicted by various other theoretical statements or definitions that he makes at other points.

In the current psychoanalytic literature, and particularly in the area known among psychoanalysts as ego psychology,[3] I see more nourishment for the kind of research, the probing, organized wondering that I am talking about. Freudian system is, after all, one of the very few comprehensive systems of description of human nature that we have. There is, however, a growing awareness of the necessity for dealing with such problems as have been left out of that system. All these good things that we can say about human beings, all that we would like to see in ourselves, is generally missing from the heart of the system. Kindness is missing, love is missing, except insofar as it can be analyzed away in a genetic sense—that is, as coming out of something lesser than itself. Nobility, sacrifice, goodness in general, virtue in general, really have no central place in the classical Freudian literature, but they are now, I think, beginning to have a place in the ego-psychological literature.

I myself have got more nourishment from the so-called neo-Freudian literature; not only the works of Fromm and Horney, but also the writings of Kurt Goldstein and Dr. Angyal,[4] which are inexcusably neglected by the psychologists, the psychiatrists, and the psychoanalysts. They deserve far more fame and widespread reading than they have yet received. I expect in about another ten years or so we will catch up with them.

This neo-Freudian revolution, which turns away from classical Freudianism, reacts against a truncated picture of the human being. The effort to put in what was missing is not necessarily a rejection of what is good in Freudianism as a system of psy-

---

[3] Various articles by E. Kris, H. Hartmann, E. Loewenstein, E. Erikson, D. Rapaport, and others.

[4] Fromm, E., *Man for Himself.* Rinehart, New York, 1947; Horney, K., *Neurosis and Human Growth.* W. W. Norton & Co., New York, 1950; Goldstein, K., *The Organism.* American Book Company, New York, 1939; Angyal, A., *Foundations for a Science of Personality.* Commonwealth Fund, New York, 1941; Moustakas, C. E., *The Self.* Harper & Bros., New York, 1956.

chopathology, its understanding of psychopathogenesis, or its technique of psychotherapy. It is possible to regard these contributions with the greatest admiration, and at the same time to understand and applaud the neo-Freudian movement. All I would call for is this superstructure that I think the neo-Freudians have been more concerned with than the Freudians.

This is the background of research, reading, and observation that leads me to the sort of thinking exemplified in the five propositions placed before you.

I would add one other point. My impression—and certainly this was true in the evolution of my own thinking and that of many other psychologists and psychiatrists—is that psychotherapy, which is our most important microscope, probably our most important technique for looking into the depths of human nature in a technical way, has to some extent been aimless, or at least has had limited goals. Under the aegis of medicine, the psychiatrists have often failed to see the hugeness of the task that psychotherapy implies. They have been content simply to get rid of sickness, that is, to make sick people not sick, while avoiding the problem of making not-sick people well, or good, or fully mature.

Within the last ten years or so, there has been a growing concern over the ultimate goals of psychotherapy. I have a bibliography of about twenty or twenty-five titles now, mostly by psychiatrists who are alert to the need for better answers. To a lesser extent I have seen this same thing paralleled in discussions—they have been pretty feeble ones so far—about the goals of education, of family life and parenthood. My own conception is that the goals of psychotherapy and the goals just mentioned are all about the same, and this, I think, is beginning to appear, too. Now, this would be one of the places, I should think, for theoretical and empirical research on the goals of psychotherapy.

One other stream of thought that is influencing me and many people I talk with flows out of the European writings, the existentialist and phenomenological writings.[5] To some extent, these are paralleled in our own country by certain of the Catholic psychologists who have been raising questions that other pyschol-

---

[5] May, R., Angel, E., Ellenberger, H. F., eds., *Existence*. Basic Books, New York, 1958; Arnold, M. B., and Gasson, J. A., eds., *The Human Person*. Ronald Press, New York, 1954; Nuttin, J., *Psychoanalysis and Personality*. Sheed and Ward, London, 1954.

ogists haven't discussed. Arnold and Gasson are names that come to my mind, and I think also of the book by Nuttin and some of the European books now being translated. These writers and writings are going to raise problems that the psychologists can say something about, not so much out of experimental work, but out of the huge mass of clinical experience that has now accumulated.

For instance, the problem of responsibility is attracting more and more attention. One of my friends coined a phrase that sticks in my mind: "This is a much-needed gap." I think that the problem of responsibility is certainly a much-needed gap. We are aware both of its gaphood and that we need very, very much to learn something about it because it is like the missing planet, which we must find before we can understand the orbits of all the other planets.

While I wouldn't speak for behavioral science (a term I dislike), I certainly would speak about much of the clinical material that is coming essentially from psychotherapy, from the study of psychopathology and psychological health. Not only do we need to work with these data, but we need also to say something about them that makes sense. The same holds true for the problems of guilt, which I won't expand on because Hobart has stressed it so strongly.

I would like to make one last point in what has turned out to be fifteen minutes instead of ten. We have a good line of research, a good technique for working with the problem of choice, at least in animals, not only in lower animals, but the higher animals, and in young human beings as well. It is certainly fair to think of life as a series of choices facing us at every moment of every day. We can elect to go in one direction or another, and I would say, for discussion purposes, that we can visualize these usually as going either in a healthward direction or in a sicknessward direction. Within the next decade or so it should be possible to adapt and apply these techniques, which are now so fine for white rats, let's say, to the problem of choice in the human being as well. That would enlarge our understanding in a most important area.

Finally, I would like to point out that many psychiatrists and psychologists, after a long look into the history of philosophy and theology, have agreed on the need to enlarge our knowledge of the whole trend toward concern with self-actualization, instead of a neo-Aristotelianism that is now coming into existence among the psychological theorists. There are enough data available to make many thoughtful psychologists find it necessary to put into their theoretical construction of the human personality something called by this name, or self-realization, or individuation, or the urge to perfection, or an urge to productiveness or creativeness.

Some months prior to the conference, Dr. Maslow was asked to submit a series of propositions as a basis for discussion. The following were submitted:

1. We psychologists are getting to know more about mature and immature religious motivations, experiences, and situations. We think that professional religionists should also face the implications of these findings.

2. The old theological problem of evil is now taking on very new aspects with advancing clinical knowledge. How much of "evil" is psychopathogenic?

3. We now have enough psychological information to criticize practically all philosophical and theological value theories that have ever been offered. These should be widely broadcast and the value theories thrown away or revised.

4. Granted that the human being is now known to have impulses to self-actualization, to growth, to maturity (all of which imply an instinct-like need for and desire for truth, goodness, beauty, etc.), why do so few people grow well in this direction? What are the evasions of growth, the blocks to growth?

5. Religious experiences, mystical experiences, and peak experiences in general have often been stigmatized as a regression to the infantile, to the womb, or to the breast. We now know that there can be, so to speak, a "regression forward" as well as a "regression backward," a union upward, as well as a union downward, a "high Nirvana," as well as a "low Nirvana." What does this mean for our conception of the good man and the good life? [6]

COMMENTS BY CHAIRMAN KLINEBERG
Dr. Maslow has given us another series of important problems to argue about. He seems to be rather more optimistic about the possibility of psychological research, if we grant him the right to interpret such research more broadly and to include clinical insights and explorations as well as straight experimentations.

---

[6] Maslow, A. H., ed., *New Knowledge in Human Values.* Harper & Bros., New York, 1958.

He spoke of the work on the good man, the noblest moment, the peak experience. If I may be permitted to throw in a question for Dr. Maslow to discuss later, is there any way of combining the psychologically felt peak experience with an objective consensus that this is a good experience? In other words, is a subjectively felt peak related to what might objectively be described as peak experience?

He raises also another aspect of Freud's position that we might add to the problem of Freud's general attitude toward religion, namely, what he describes, if I am not quoting incorrectly, as "the contradictory, nonsensical theory of love." That forthright phrasing may raise some pro-Freudian hackles and provoke some argument and discussion among others here.

He suggests new goals for psychotherapy, which I suppose might not be too far removed—I would like him later, if he will, to comment on it—from those the World Health Organization tried to insist on when it said that health was not just the absence of disease, but a positive state of well-being.

And he mentions the contributions by a number of writers whom perhaps most of us in psychology don't consult often enough. These include not only the neo-Freudians but Catholic and other writers who have dealt with problems that Dr. Maslow thinks we have neglected in the usual kind of psychology that we teach or on which we do research. He himself has indicated the belief that research is possible on some of these fundamental, important questions.

DISCUSSION
In the general discussion that followed, a priest expressed the feeling that neither speaker had adequately considered the nature of man or had said enough about religion or mental health. "What *is* man's nature, and what is his goal? Does he have a purpose? Does he have a goal within himself?" He took issue with a statement made that "religion gives to man." "A really mature religion," he said, "doesn't give anything to man; it is a service to God." He agreed with Dr. Mowrer that science, at least science's measuring and observing techniques, would not help much in studying the role of religion. Value systems had been attacked as being unscientific, lacking data to back them up. Freud and his followers for years had gone along without anything but introspective data, and they were attacked for that.

There are other tools available for studying the nature of man—deductive reasoning, for example. This speaker made a plea for a diversified approach to the study of man, with careful examination of different points of view and with the recognition that little is known about man's emotions in sickness and in health.

A psychiatrist spoke in emphatic disagreement with Dr. Mowrer's statements to the effect that religion, at the end of the nineteenth century, had almost gone down under the onslaught of scientific discoveries but had made a strong recovery. As an instance, he cited the destruction by bombing of the monastery at Monte Cassino, an event that caused great and widespread distress. An atheist friend of the speaker had pointed out that the ancient abbey had been completely destroyed three times before. "To him, Monte Cassino was an indestructible fact, and all the other things were passing phases."

Stressing the need for extreme clarity of statement, the psychiatrist continued: "Reference was made to organized religion. Are organized religion and religion the same thing? I doubt it. Are religious experiences and organized semiliturgical and liturgical ceremonies the same things? Now, if we don't speak of these things clearly, we will not know what we are talking about. We know that there are very healthy men and women who are frightful people, people who just don't care about a thing. So let's not confuse ethical values with mental health, religion with organized religion. Sometimes they coincide. And at the same time, let's not confuse the rise and fall of religion with the sound of the cannonade during the war. Maybe at that time religion was at its highest; we don't know."

This speaker disagreed with Dr. Maslow's estimate of the importance of the contribution of European existentialist writers on the ground that in America they had offered little, and that in Europe existentialism by itself was a far different thing from existentialism partly wedded to psychology. There is confusion about the meaning of existentialism except when it is considered as a philosophy. The same psychiatrist also questioned the value of neo-Freudianism, which he considered to be an attempt to philosophize without knowing philosophy, with loss of clinical perspective.

"When people talk about goodness and maturity and mental health and schizophrenia," he continued, "I feel really terribly confused. So was Freud when he said that religion saved people from neurosis, and that only saints—and he quoted Saint Francis —could escape a neurosis. This confusion of mental health, goodness, and highest and noblest experiences is a very dangerous thing."

Another participant remarked almost gleefully upon the problems of communication that had cropped up so far in the discussion, and said that these and others that might follow would, in his opinion, alone justify the holding of the conference. He added that the great limitation upon the study of man is that the only available instrument for that study is man himself. Therefore, it is necessary to specify from what perspective and with what microscope one is looking at man.

At this point, Dr. Klineberg stepped out of his role as chairman and entered the discussion. He agreed that the problem of communication was serious, but thought that possibly even more dangerous were dogmatic inferences drawn by members of the different disciplines. "If I understood some of you correctly," he said, "you are telling us that understanding has been reached. I don't think we can reach an agreement if, on the one hand, we feel that this is something that needs exploring and in connection with which we still have a long way to go, and if, on the other hand, we are told, 'No, you can stop this because the answers are already there.' I don't think that would make psychologists very happy."

Another symposium member agreed, urging the necessity of defining frames of reference and making other semantic differentiations. "Is psychology here a method? Is it tending along certain lines? To what points does it feel its authority extends? At another point, where does it really enter into the value systems? I think if we could get some clarification here, it would be useful. I suggest to both Dr. Mowrer and Dr. Maslow that it would be of value if they would define the area of sickness or psychological unhealthiness, and then perhaps we, on the other hand, might say, 'What is this in terms of our religious orientation?' " He pointed out that in religion as in other fields one may learn about the positive by looking at the negative, just as one examines the abnormal to find the normal.

"I heartily agree," said one of the psychologists, "with the need for definition of the nature of man. I am distrustful of either-ors, and I think that sometimes there is a kind of reaction formation occurring on both sides of the fence—on the empirical and the deductive side. I think that the behavioral sciences have been somewhat guilty of defensive action in feeling that in order to measure up to 'science' they have had to outdo the empiricists. On the other hand, I think that we have to recognize that in the nature of our quest there are many problems that cannot be solved empirically. I would make a plea, therefore, that we approach this problem from both sides."

Dr. Maslow expressed the conviction that there are no "either-ors" today, and that if the truth is the truth, it will all come out in the wash. He pointed out that empiricism frequently merely confirms things that have been known for millenia. Even disagreements can be valuable, he said. "If there are at any one moment contradictions between the sum total of 'scientific truth' and deductive or philosophic or theological conclusions, then even this is advantageous, I should think, on both sides. It would cause the philosophers to re-examine their own theoretical conclusions from the data so that there would be a mutually corrective kind of feedback."

Discussion turned upon the possibility of a theory of love. Someone had said that Freud had no knowledge of love. A participant quoted Freud as having said specifically that to him *libido* came to mean *eros*, and he used *eros* in the sense of love. The speaker preferred to use *eros* in the Platonic sense, in the sense of the apostle Paul's words to the Corinthians, in the sense of *caritas*.

A speaker questioned the belief that psychology is in a period of revolution, principally because of Freud's contribution; he noted that the theory of the unconscious had been enunciated some years before Freud.

Throughout the discussion at this first session, the emphasis was upon the potentialities and the limitations of psychology as a means of studying the human being. A conclusion reached at several points was the need for a multiple approach. This would require, it was agreed, a broad study of the relations between the "empirical-inductive method" and the "deductive method"— whether they are in opposition or may be mutually helpful.

As you know, the theory of personality that we have now in general is really an extrapolation from the study of illness; a sort of reverse proposition. Health, psychological health, or that which is desirable in the human being, is very frequently defined by psychiatrists, and especially by the Freudian psychiatrists, as simply the absence of illness or the relief of symptoms or the cessation of a particular kind of misery, although Freud himself sometimes got pessimistic about that, too. There are passages in Freud in which it looks as if all that human beings could hope for was to change acute misery for just normal suffering, as he once called it.

I just don't understand why this kind of work hasn't been done by others. Of course, there are difficulties that arise, such as the untrustworthiness of the experimental data by ordinary criteria of validity, when one person, one human being, selects and studies the people he admires. This is full of pitfalls and booby traps, yet I would suggest that other people try to do the same sort of thing—again in a naturalistic and descriptive way, in a primitive scientific way. It needn't be fancy at all. It is just the study of the finest people we can pick out.

Now, to me this has been extremely rewarding. It has unsettled my whole attitude toward psychology in practically every department. One accepted law after another has crashed for me in the last decade or two as a result of this kind of research. You may call it primitive research, or prescientific research, and still the possibilities are wide open. Much of what I have to say comes from the study of such people.

Secondly, another kind of work that is possible—I know it is possible because I have done it—is the study of the highest moments, those moments in human life in which the person is seen at his best, at his noblest, at his finest, when he reaches the fullest heights he is capable of attaining.[2] This started out in various ways. I was much interested, during the course of my first work in studying very healthy, mature, well-developed human beings, to find that such a large proportion of them reported to me that they had what sounded very much like the mystic experiences that William James described, that the whole mystic literature has described. I pursued this tack.

I was also interested in the aesthetic and the creative experi-

---

[2] Maslow, A. H., "Cognition of Being in the Peak-experiences." *Journal of Genetic Psychology*, 1959, *94,* first half, March, 43.

ence. I did some researches on the love need and the love experience, and then I found these coming together. These were all high moments in the life of the individual, and I found it possible, finally, to generalize them all and to seek out a subjective experience—I called it the peak experience—summarizing all the moments in which the human being is at his peak; when he is transiently healthy and noble and wonderful and fine. This work is still under way and I keep finding more and more kinds of experiences, more and more paths to this kind of subjective experience in which the person not only changes momentarily but the whole personality may get reorganized permanently.

A question that you are all familiar with is religious conversion, but there are other kinds of conversions, it now turns out, in which the character structure of the person changes. His *Weltanschauung,* or cognition of the world, changes, and the resulting perspicuity or the penetration to depths of reality that such people have never attained before simply makes it possible for them forever after to see reality, the world, the cosmos, in a different way altogether.

Now, I would advance the proposition that this is properly scientific work, at least in the historical sense, even if it doesn't come up to the standards that psychologists have got used to when they are handling relatively simpler problems. It is work, probing, research—organized curiosity, if you want to call it that —strictly naturalistic in the sense of calling on no variables outside the system of observation itself. It is possible for it to be objective because, more and more, we do have techniques for laying aside our own hopes and wishes—that is, the hopes and wishes and fears of the observer. Moreover, science is a self-cleansing procedure. It can be checked by other people doing the same thing; that is, by people with other wishes, other hopes and other fears, so that the necessary corrections can be made.

Regarding the study of the love experience, I may say that I had naïvely followed the general conception of Freud, who frequently has been called the philosopher of love, the great psychologist of love. When I examined Freud's works more carefully, and reviewed the whole psychoanalytic index that makes this possible—collating all that Freud had said about love and all that I could find by other psychoanalysts—I found it was the most arrant nonsense possible to conceive. If you can get them

ORIENTATION SESSION

Members of the first symposium attended an informal orientation session on Friday afternoon, December 6th. Dr. Kenneth E. Appel, president of the Academy, presided. After welcoming the guests, he introduced Dr. Harvey J. Tompkins, Chairman of the Committee on Arrangements.

Dr. Tompkins said that the discussions to follow were to be only preliminary to the first steps the Academy would take on its way toward its objectives. The committee hoped that no one would feel under any compulsion to try to arrive at definite conclusions or "all-encompassing recommendations." Continuing such conferences through the years was the committee's plan, carrying forward the discussions initiated here, and enlarging upon whatever suggestions might come out of these meetings. Memberships of future conferences would not be exactly the same as this one, but would vary according to the subject matter.

The committee hoped for a continuous spirit of informality throughout the sessions. To this end, it had planned the program with the smallest degree of structure possible. Outside the meeting hours, members were free to do as they pleased—gather in small groups for further talk, walk about the grounds, or just go to their rooms.

Dr. Appel sketched in the outlines of the mental health problem. It is known to be the nation's number one public health problem in size and severity. The number of people being admitted to mental hospitals in this country is staggering—larger than the population of some of the nations that have contributed significantly to Western culture. Our economy will be carrying the burden of its damage for many years to come. The cost of emotional and mental illness in terms of human happiness is incalculable. The vast material accomplishments of the Western World, its technological advances, even its accumulation of book knowledge are not enough to assure the happiness of our people.

We have some 325,000 clergymen in the United States, Dr. Appel said, and somewhat more than 100 million people who say they are affiliated with some religious group. The clergy are involved in helping people to live full and effective lives. The psychiatrists, of whom there are fewer than 10,000 in the country, are involved in the restoration and preservation of health, and in preventing some of the things that are distressing in our society. The two disciplines share a common concern. It is, therefore, understandable and appropriate for the psychiatrist to be interested in religion and the motivations and attitudes of people toward their fellows. Recent happenings have shown us that our concern must extend even beyond our own little globe.

Following these comments, Dr. Appel asked the members of the conference to identify themselves and to say a few words about their backgrounds and special interests.

The president voiced the Academy's gratitude to the Josiah Macy, Jr. Foundation for its financial support of the conference and for the understanding co-operation of its medical director, Dr. Frank Fremont-Smith.

In his turn, Dr. Fremont-Smith reminded his hearers that a foundation is always correspondingly grateful for an opportunity to put its funds into rewarding undertakings. He spoke of the Macy Foundation's early interest in the relation between religion and medical science, taking substance in the 1930's in assistance to the Committee on Religion and Health of the New York Academy of Medicine.

It is not easy for different branches of the behavioral sciences

CONTRIBUTIONS AND RESPONSIBILITIES OF THE

BEHAVIORAL SCIENCES AND MEDICINE

WITH SPECIAL EMPHASIS

ON PSYCHIATRY

CHAIRMAN
Harvey J. Tompkins, M.D.

DISCUSSION LEADERS
Gregory Zilboorg, M.D.
Harold G. Wolff, M.D.

CONTRIBUTIONS AND RESPONSIBILITIES OF THE

BEHAVIORAL SCIENCES AND MEDICINE

WITH SPECIAL EMPHASIS

ON PSYCHIATRY

INTRODUCTION BY CHAIRMAN TOMPKINS

At the conclusion of our session last evening, Dr. Klineberg said we would have an opportunity to pursue the very pertinent topics brought forward in that meeting. Every one of these meetings will provide such an opportunity. In each session a new area will be opened up, but our discussion will not be limited to it. There must be continuity, so we will go backwards and forwards. Certainly last evening psychiatry was mentioned. In this session it will be introduced more or less formally.

If I may speak personally for a moment, I should like to say that, in common with many of my colleagues, I have been abruptly faced with some impediments to progress through the mutual suspicion on the part of psychiatry and religion. I decline to believe, as some do, that this is necessary. I think it comes about only through lack of understanding by psychiatrists and religionists of each other's roles and objectives. This is true in the case of the social sciences in general, as well as for psychiatry.

To facilitate discussion, I shall ask our discussion leaders to limit their presentations to ten minutes, if possible, and I suggest that we pause after the first presentation for discussion before we hear the second.

PRESENTATION BY DR. ZILBOORG

The discussion of the relationship between religion and psychiatry has gained considerable momentum during the past few years. There is always a place for contention in human relations, particularly in the case of those of our prejudices and predilections that we like to call convictions. Good and well-meaning minds occasionally assume that it is all a matter of words, or a way of telling one another what one means—since the last war we are wont to speak of this difficulty as the problem of communication. As if to say: if the psychiatrist could tell us clearly what he means, and the clergyman could tell us clearly what he means, they would be sure to solve the many problems they have in common.

I am sorry to say that I am not an adherent of the communication theory, which tends to become more and more a practice of popularized disciplines (both scientific and theological) made anemic enough to become almost lifeless and transparent enough to become invisible. The fact that I know nothing, literally nothing, about the serology of encephalitis does not make me doubt the serious worker in the field. I need no special overstrained simplification of "communication" to understand that scientific worker with my heart, respect his efforts, and even accept his results if and when such are forthcoming.

The issues before us are really more direct and more simple. The psychiatrist—and by this I mean the psychotherapist and not the speculative, philosophical psychiatrist—must of necessity know man in his totality; he must look upon the human person as one and indivisible, and avoid those pseudo-convenient dichotomies that traditionally divide man into a body and a soul. We must not forget that *soul* in the theological sense is not within the purview of the psychotherapist. True, the psychotherapist must take into consideration the transcending spiritual aspects of his patient's personality, but as long as he is a psychotherapist he is not concerned with those aspects directly. When one fixes one's gaze on the north to study the aurora borealis, one does not forget that there is a south, nor does one disregard its existence; but it is north that one is studying, and for all practical purposes the south is for the time being none of one's business.

All this may sound too dogmatic, but in actuality it is not. The surgeon who watches the signs of ebb and flow of life at the operating table keeps on doing his job to save and maintain life without making or even perceiving any reference to the theological value of life or the metaphysical significance of the struggle for physiological survival.

In all the discussions I have heard or taken part in on the relationship between religion and psychiatry or clinical psychology, here and in Europe, I have found the same singular error of trying to make the psychiatrist a borderline theologian, and the theologian a borderline, but preferably a full-fledged, clinical psychologist. These efforts do not bid fair to increase the efficacy of "communication" between the psychiatrist and the clergyman. I always was and still am—and I am afraid I always shall be—suspicious of tying psychiatric problems in with religious ones, as if these two fields really have something in common. This is the reason why I am skeptical about the tendency, perhaps unspoken but put in evidence in considerable relief, to connect mental health and religious life. If you are very ill mentally, you can't be a halfway decent street cleaner any more than lead a proper religious life; yet capital criminals may have a religious life of considerable depth, and neurotics can achieve sainthood. I feel like warning myself to beware when emphasis is laid on the fact that religious life promotes mental health, and good old mental health promotes religious life.

It suffices and it must be known that whatever depths are

plumbed by the psychoanalysts or penetrated by clergymen, in the end man must be found to be a mystery honestly and reverently recognized by all. This is the reason why I am unable to lay particular stress on the unconscious motivation of asymptomatic human behavior. If I am a good dishwasher, I wash dishes well, and it is of no earthly or unearthly importance whether I wash dishes well as an overcompensatory reaction against my unconscious desire to break the many dishes my mother used to wash, or whether it is because out of love of my dear mother I want by way of unconscious identification to do as good a job of dishwashing as she did when I was a kid and watched her in the kitchen.

As you see, as long as religious life is moderately what people call by that very vague term normal, I see no particular value in tying it up with its connections in the reservoir of the unconscious. This is essentially the reason why Freud was in error when he pointed out that religion can be explained by the unconscious, infantile gratifications that religion, or its practice, provides. As long as man remains a living being, there will always be endless and innumerable connections between our highest conscious functioning and our darkest and flimsiest infantile unconscious life. We cannot expect that a beautiful, healthy tree has roots without worms or anaerobic micro-organisms around them.

The confusion between unconscious trends and their corresponding normal trends is a real confusion created by the present-day popularization of the psychology of the unconscious, which became popular, indeed, and misunderstood in proportion to its popularity.

The real issue is how to differentiate between the psychological and the spiritual and not confuse one's psychological with one's spiritual life. Not that these two are separated with a wall that cannot be penetrated. It is true that that wall is a mystery, and it cannot be penetrated by our empirical, positivistic psychology; but we must also remember that the transcending aspects of man cannot be measured by scientific tests or such shibboleths as maturity or adjustment.

The rapprochement between the theologian and the psychiatrist is possible only if both will recognize the validity of either.

DISCUSSION

The first person to speak, a psychologist, observed that religionists were interested in two phases of life: the philosophical, involving credo, and the practical, or pastoral, having to do with the self-realization and self-fulfillment of the people in their charge. He said that he was interested in people being good, and also in *why* they are good. He thought that people may conform to certain ethical standards because they are defending themselves against strong desires of evil—"that is, they may really be evil, but they want to give the impression of being good." This is a question of mental health. He believed it was most important that the "why" of people's goodness be brought home to them, that they be made to realize the action formation of their goodness. In any discussion of this subject, it seemed to him that the aspect of religion must here be recognized.

Another symposium member asked whether Dr. Zilboorg had meant to say that he considered it pointless to bring theologians and psychiatrists together in search of a common ground on which to work. He doubted that the subject matters of the two fields are actually as sharply separated as Dr. Zilboorg had indicated, for the examples selected to illustrate the differences between their concerns—the concepts of soul and immortality—are indeed points where it is extremely difficult for them to come together. There are other broad concepts of mutual interest to the two disciplines, such as the concept of isolation.

Dr. Zilboorg asked whether the speaker was using the term "isolation" in a theological or a psychological sense, whereupon another participant said that Dr. Zilboorg was proposing a dichotomy. Man, said this speaker, is a totality and has to be taken as a whole; he regarded Dr. Zilboorg's attempt to demarcate the religious and mental aspects of personality as an error.

"It seems to me," said a clergyman-psychologist, "that one of the common things that might bring us together is that no matter how we approach this—as psychologists, as I might, or as a clergyman, as I might, or as psychiatrists, as some of the others here might—we are faced with mystery. We are all groping with various tools, and this is where we sometimes misunderstand each other, because we don't always understand our tools or agree with their validities. It seems to me that we are not necessarily dividing the theme—we are instead rather approaching it from different variations of similar methodologies, or from quite different methodologies.

"I am thinking now of the psychologist's anxiety to validate things mathematically in many instances. This forces him to many extremes of experimentation and even of simplification to obtain his validations, which a more sensitive clinical kind of person, as a psychiatrist would be, might not see any reason to do.

"I think the clergyman may not see the point in this kind of thing, either, because he will have neither the clinician's point of view nor the scientist's mathematicized point of view. We may say these are not good points of view, but it seems to me they represent the areas we can grow to understand one another in. It is not necessarily that we are dealing with different things absolutely. But it seems to me we have a rather complex problem here: different methodologies, different language of communication, and different ways of viewing the same thing."

Another priest-psychologist asked for clarification of a basic principle of psychoanalysis, the pleasure principle. "I wonder if it is possible," he said, "to isolate a theory of the psyche from the general conception of what human happiness is. I think that when Freud explains the passages of the pleasure principle, the reality principle, he again raises a distinction that may exist between pleasure and joy. Joy always implies some thought of rational factors, because we may have plenty of joy in doing something that is not pleasurable, and we may have pleasure where there is no joy. If we do something, for instance, looking only for pleasure that our conscience may not approve of, we may have pleasure without any joy. We may have joy in accomplishing something that is totally lacking in pleasure. So I think that possibly from the very beginning of our interpretation of the human psyche, even on the deterministic level, we must be aware of what happens, and this implies some philosophical consideration."

Another member of the group asked Dr. Zilboorg to comment on one aspect of Freud's criticism of religion. "I find it rather difficult to believe that even though Freud did not philosophize in any systematic sense, there weren't great implications for philosophy as well as for religion in what he said. For example, it seems to me that the most important aspect of Freud's criticism of religion is that it focuses infantile dependency needs, that it induces them, disseminates them, and preserves them. Now, if you follow this implication, he was creating in a scientific sense a new concept of man, one that modern psychiatry has produced in its concept of maturity: that man, mature man, is perhaps not self-reliant in the Emersonian sense, but that he can stand in some manner upon his own two feet, upon his own resources. The question I would pose to Dr. Zilboorg is, would he agree that religion in some manner fosters infantile needs? At what point does religion, in his opinion, produce—to use a psychiatric concept—maturity?"

Dr. Zilboorg responded vigorously. "You have said, by implication—both in philosophy and in religion—that religion, according to Freud, is a result of, or an expression of, infantile dependency needs. You ask whether I would agree that religion *fosters* infantile dependency. But Freud never said that. There is a difference between expression of a need and something fostering that need. . . .

"What's wrong with our being dependent on God like children? To give ourselves completely, with the complete faith with which an infant gives himself to the mother or father—this is a pattern of infancy, but it is not infantile; it is a mistake to believe that.

"It is a mistake to believe that a beautiful tree growing magnificently in our garden must be so sterile and clean that you will not find a single worm at its roots. If you don't find worms, the worms will not eat up things that will not rot, and you will have bad soil and the beautiful tree will be gone. Roots have worms. . . .

"But we are simplifying the thing too much. I really am frankly and openly impatient with the kind of reasoning that says: 'All human beings are mortal; frogs are mortal; therefore, frogs are human beings.' It just doesn't go like that.

"Freud immensely illuminated the sources of our development, but by 'maturity' he did not mean that when a man is married he makes up a schedule of marital relations, and when he has children he makes up a schedule of when the children will read and when they will talk. No! We still live spontaneously, and a human embrace must have all the qualities of human passion and love; if it doesn't, it isn't living. And God didn't mean it that way."

Dr. Zilboorg returned to the earlier statement by a symposium member to the effect that he had said that psychiatry and religion had nothing in common. "There are certain things on which we could get together. I don't say that the theologian should be totally separated from the psychiatrist. A psychiatrist who wants to be a theologian can become one. It would be good for him. If a theologian wants to become a psychiatrist, he ought to have a medical degree. . . .

"The main issue is that I am not dividing the personality of man. I am not violating the unity and the indivisibility of the human person, whether it has soma or doesn't have soma. Before you eat your bread it is separate, but once you have consumed it, it is part of you in totality.

"You asked me about isolation," Dr. Zilboorg continued to another participant. "You had an excellent idea, but I'm glad you said that you don't confuse that with the phenomenon and mechanism of isolation. The isolation of man, which Freud so beautifully described—the peculiar loneliness—has its emotional concomitants and components, but they are the mechanics. The purely philosophical implications of a sense of isolation are different from the purely psychological ones. At the psychological level, being isolated may mean that we love nobody or we hate everybody, whereas being isolated in the theological sense means being isolated from God. You might feel even like Christ, Who for a moment felt isolated from God on the Cross before He gave up the Ghost. It is very important."

Turning to another aspect of the same subject, Dr. Zilboorg said: "Freud never wanted to seek happiness. Joy, it is true, isn't happiness; but joy, which means feeling oneself in harmony with the rest of the world, is the abandonment of the sense of isolation, even when you suffer. This is an important point that requires considerable study, but it is not, strictly speaking, a psychological issue."

PRESENTATION BY DR. WOLFF

I would like, in these few minutes, to present a simplified statement of a theory of disease. I am going to do this by showing you the kind of evidence on which this theory has been put together, and something about its development. If I am successful, I shall leave you with the idea that disease is an aspect of adaptation, and I assume that adaptation, for man, would have fundamental religious implications.

Some fifteen or more years ago, while first working on problems of pain, I was much impressed by the fact that many of the reactions of an individual experiencing pain were far away from the site of injury. There seemed to be a heterogeneous jumble of physiological responses that made no particular pattern. But as one looked at these reactions, it became clearer that they were part of some over-all adaptive reaction by the individual in his attempts to deal with the effects of harmful stimulation, or pain. That is to say, they were often mobilization reactions. (I use "mobilization" in the sense that the individual assembles his forces to get away from the damaging experience, or to attack it.)

Having arrived at such a conception of reactions to pain, I was then impressed, as I worked with frightened people, to see that in many cases these very same reactions of mobilization were present when persons were not actually experiencing the sensation of pain, but were reacting to something in their environment that was of an extremely threatening nature. This threatening factor was most often some symbol of danger, a symbol of a danger experienced in the past, or of danger to some important interpersonal relationship, or of danger to the fulfillment of individual needs, goals, and purposes.

I inferred that, since man is a goal-directed creature and his defenses rather limited, the latter may be used without precise discrimination and not necessarily most effectively. To test this point of view there began a series of observations on persons who offered special opportunities. For example, we were able to examine what happened to a man's stomach, because his stomach had had to be externalized through an opening in the abdominal wall at an early age after an injury to his esophagus. We could look at the membranes of the stomach during his various day-to-day life experiences and adjustments. It became clear that there were two extremes of reaction in the stomach. One occurred when the person felt overwhelmed; the whole digestive process stopped. The second type, an overactivity of the digestive process, occurred when he did not feel overwhelmed by a threatening circumstance, or symbols of threat, but became energized to meet it, or was aggressive in his relation to it.

This concept raised other questions. Was the pattern of response always one of fight or flight, or mobilization for action, or were there patterns evoked by symbols that had to do with building-up processes, preparation for what lay beyond a crisis—the pattern, for example, that would be associated with the taking of food? In other words, under certain circumstances this person perceived as threatening—not a situation that you or I might think of as threatening, but one that seemed so to him—his stomach would act as though he were about to eat. At first it seemed curious that a person under threatening circumstances would use a pattern having to do with eating, but then I was reminded of other instances in nature, cases of animals presenting what might be called displaced patterns. Naturalists have observed that herring gulls, for example, in a situation calling for either the aggressive action of fighting or flying away in retreat and being unable to do either, would start pulling grass. Now, grass pulling has to do with nest building, so the gull in conflict between fight or flight resorted to the building of a nest.

In a stepwise fashion, we examined other organs besides the stomach. We had an opportunity to study a series of persons each of whom, because of intractable colitis, had had his large bowel externalized. We saw, under circumstances perceived as threatening by these individuals, patterns of ejection such as might be seen when one had inadvertently swallowed a poisonous material.

In the case of the airways, we saw many persons, again in reaction to situations that they perceived as threatening, who would shut out, neutralize, wash away, by means of swelling and secretions in their upper airways, situations that couldn't possibly be dealt with in this way. Devices that were useful for shutting out and washing away dust, micro-organisms, or irritant gases, were evoked under circumstances having to do with interpersonal relationships in which the individual might not wish to participate.

We examined a kidney, and found that its blood flow alternately increased or decreased under circumstances of threat that could hardly be conceived of as needfully evoking such reactions. Or the blood pressure would rise or fall as though the individual were preparing for some crisis that, indeed, wasn't evident as he quietly sat in his chair.

In many persons there would be a painful, sustained contraction of muscles as part of a reaction of defense or preparation for assault when the antagonist was not even clearly identifiable.

And most recently, in a study of the brain and its functions, an attempt has been made to understand whether this master organ of adaptation, being involved in all of these untoward and inappropriate responses to situations perceived as threatening, may not itself be damaged during prolonged circumstances of frustration, deprivation, and postponement. I am prepared now to say, after four years of inquiry, that I am convinced that the brain may be damaged in the process of attempting to make adaptations to situations that the individual cannot meet.

If, then, these organs and organ systems are used under circumstances that are not appropriate for them to be implicated in, how does one relate this to a theory of disease? I will try to put it together for you and then show you the further evidence for the thesis.

The goal-directed individual who fails to attain his goals calls upon a number of adaptive devices. These defenses are evident in both behavior and attitude. For example, he pretends the situation is other than it is. He jokes and clowns and denies. He blames others or something outside himself. He explains away or rationalizes or puts his failure in the category of abstraction, where it is less offensive. He becomes overly busy in directions that are not appropriate but that nevertheless accord immediate satisfactions and therefore tranquilize or temporarily allow him to continue in his threatened state; or failing in any or all of these, he may invoke that most ominous one, the depersonalization pattern in which an individual figuratively pulls down the curtain and acts as if he cannot see the danger. Failing in all of these defenses, he may then pass through a state that I have called, for lack of a better word, one of nonadaptation or the "unadapted phase." This is an extremely dangerous state, in which the person's defenses are operating only intermittently and in which he is aware of an uneasy, insecure, or anxious feeling, in which his thinking is slowed and impaired, in which his capacity to make a decision as to direction and activity seems to be blocked. In such a state he may evoke one or more of the bodily patterns that I have just reviewed for you. With their continued and inappropriate use under circumstances that they cannot in themselves modify or alter, the end result is tissue damage. In the case of the stomach, where an eating pattern is used too long, the individual erodes his own mucous membrane. In the case of the bowel, where the person is "ejecting" his unresolvable threats, he also damages the overengorged mucous membrane. In the case of the upper airways, again he damages the mucous membranes of the turbinates and the air passages and makes a propitious environment for infective agents. In the case of the kidneys, he interferes with the circulation and creates situations relevant to hypertension and ultimate nephritis, uremia, and death. In the case of the brain, he starts a process in which more and more over-all adaptive versatility is lost. This state may be called by various names, but its end result is deterioration of highest-level function.

Now, how pertinent are these observations? What evidence is there that they are of importance on a large scale? In a survey of some 3,500 ostensibly well persons, we attempted to find out what periods of their lives were periods of health, and what were periods of disease, and what portion of the population made up the sick. A few generalizations immediately followed. About a quarter to a third of this group composed of 3,300 Americans, 100 Chinese, and 100 Hungarians were responsible for between 50 and 75 per cent of the total amount of illness. The length of illness, for example in a very large group of some 2,000 persons studied by my associate, Dr. Hinkle, with health records extending over twenty years, varied from twenty days of absence in twenty years to 1,300 days of absence in twenty years. Impressive was the fact that the list of illnesses encompassed a wide variety of diagnoses. The most ill were ill as regards mood, thought, and behavior; they were ill with diseases called medical, with diseases called surgical, and often with diseases called social.

Interestingly enough, their periods of illness clustered. There were periods when there were many illnesses; there were periods when there were few or none. The periods when there were more illnesses included the bulk of minor and a certain number of major illnesses.

We then attempted to find out whether the periods of greater illness and lesser illness were in any way related to how the individuals perceived themselves in their environment at the time. We came out with the generalization that the most sick were those who saw themselves as almost continually threatened, who felt dissatisfied, frustrated, disappointed, discouraged. They were conscientious, thoughtful, but troubled people. The most well, on the other hand, were people who felt relatively satisfied with what had been handed out to them and what they had done with it, who felt that they had had the "breaks" and that they had made the most of them. They were less troubled, less anxious.

My personal opinion was that the least ill were not necessarily the most attractive human beings. The least ill were sometimes more than acceptably detached and indifferent to human suffering, were lacking in human compassion, and were among those who "did not stand up to be counted."

There is a small group not yet carefully studied. They are the giants of creative energy who live long and active lives, who have the gifts and the energy to create situations wherein they can operate effectively and make the most of their gifts.

To epitomize, I am of the opinion that illness or disease is an aspect of adaptation, that at its simplest level this represents an over- or undershooting of the mark of certain adaptive arrangements that are on the whole appropriate. What happens in a lung when it mobilizes its forces against an invading pneumococcus? Extra amounts of blood and large numbers of protective white blood cells accumulate and congest the part. We call that pneumonia. Such a protective-adaptive reaction is, on the whole, making too much of a good thing, but this is the kind of disease that begins as a response of an appropriate sort and overshoots the mark. But when a person uses his stomach as part of a reaction to symbols of what he perceives as threatening, then his response may be both inappropriate and excessive. The inappropriateness as well as the quantity of reaction lead to disease.

It is obvious, then, that direction, pressures, goals, values are relevant to the problems of disease, both at the level of the brain and at the level of the other body organs, at the level of the mind and that of secretion.

Of course, when I introduce the concept of morality into this, it must be understood that the good is not necessarily the readily understandable, that there is a need for constant penetration into the order in nature to perceive it, so that what is truly good for man can be understood and become a part of the adaptive process he is called upon to make.

DISCUSSION

One of the psychiatrists opened the discussion by asking if Dr. Wolff had been referring to automatic functioning of the stomach rather than conscious, deliberate use.

Dr. Wolff replied that what he had been talking about was well beyond the level of conscious use, and added: "I would like to emphasize that the conscious and unconscious hardly need to be gone into. We assume that much of man's activity is unconscious, and certainly the use of these parts and these patterns is often enough unconscious."

Referring to the health-illness survey that Dr. Wolff had described, a member of the group asked: "Is there any kind of bridge between the concern of religion and religious leaders who are interested in this general goal and a feeling of security and satisfaction? When you looked at your 3,500 patients and were able to separate a group of those who were regularly healthy and those who were regularly unhealthy, were you able to find some of these particular aspects that are related to a general religious faith or a feeling of security? Or did any of them get that out of ethical principles or a general optimistic make-up, which you may be able to explain but which we often have to take for granted?"

"The common denominator of those who were most well," answered Dr. Wolff, "was, as I tried to imply, a kind of workable relationship to the world they lived in, or preferred to live in, in contrast to those who did not achieve such a relationship. I don't think I would like to draw any inferences from that. It is conceivable that there were common denominators in the various kinds of workable relationships, but I am not prepared to discuss that."

Another symposium member wanted clarification of the import of the findings derived from the survey. "Dr. Wolff, if I understand you, the implication was also that those who were adaptable, who you said were the least sick, were not always the most attractive of human beings. Now, one can draw the inference that the healthy need not necessarily be the moral or the ethical. By reverse connotation, the ethical and moral may be so highly sensitive as always to get sick, or, shall we say, to be sick-prone. Now, what is the relationship here between health and morality, or, if I may reduce this to an absurdity, is health a lack of morality?"

Dr. Wolff agreed that this was partially so. "If you will allow me again to oversimplify it, I think to be a good human being is to be a little sick. Of course, personal survival is only a small part of the human goal-directed activity. First and last, the human is a tribe-oriented or group-oriented creature, and freedom from pain, freedom from discomfort, and personal survival are ancillary to these over-all purposes. His obliteration may be necessary to the fulfillment of his conception of himself, and therefore sickness isn't necessarily the central topic."

"I wonder," asked a psychiatrist, "taking this group of pretty healthy people and this other group, if the common factor may not be the degree of discrepancy or consistency between the accepted goals and the behavior. If the goals are simple, not very far-reaching, then it's easier to be consistent than when one has higher goals; there is less discrepancy."

Dr. Wolff agreed with this idea, and gave an example. "A housewife who had more demands for herself and her children and a fairly high conception of what her place in life should be would be sicker than one who had a marriage that wasn't going well. The latter woman would have retired from it, made no demands for herself or her life, and might be perfectly happy living a routine life as a telephone operator, let's say. I think you are right, and that there is a discrepancy between what is available and what the individual expects out of his experience, and that the one who is aware of the discrepancy is more likely to be associated with the kind of abreaction that is called illness."

A participant remarked that, although human beings react to stimuli with the organs of the body in a way that no other creatures do, all human beings do not so react in the same degree. Some people, hysterical persons, for example, tend to convert psychic pains into bodily pains and tensions more than others do. Perhaps, he suggested, absence of responsibility may be better for a person. Those who are ill pay for it either with their muscles or with anxiety. But the more infantile person is certainly one who has never reached a certain level; like the psychopath, he may be breeding more illnesses than the more concerned and responsible person is. The child is absolved of responsibility that will later cause psychosomatic illness. Then there is another group that Dr. Wolff had mentioned, "the exceptionally creative and zestful people, who do not have the generalized neurotic tendency to confuse reality with fantasy, but are able to accept the nature of reality without projecting into it after-misinterpretations or present symbolic misinterpretations."

One of the psychiatrists commented on the relation between mental and physical illness, saying: "In the big state institutions where provision is made for medical and surgical illnesses, they have all had this experience. When very sick people, deteriorated schizophrenics and wildly mentally sick people, contract a physical illness and are brought into the hospital, they behave very quietly, as if they were not mentally sick; and they begin to vituperate as they get physically better. Apparently we deal here with a form of adaptation of the individual to his organism in illness or, as Freud said, apparently we deal with the amount that needs to be withdrawn for the ego or for other purposes.

"I was wondering whether the conclusions that Dr. Wolff offers us do not have a much more profound implication. Is it not true that the amount of psychic energy we possess is our capital, and that it cannot be increased or decreased? We can only display how much we spend, but the capital remains constant within a given individual.

"The moment we deal with an illness that is the result of adaptation, the adaptation becomes automatic, even if the type of adaptation no longer serves any purpose. The amount of psychic energy is withdrawn and concentrated at those parts of the human personality, including the body, that are affected, and very much less is left."

Why is it, this participant asked, that some very sick people are extraordinarily creative and brilliant? "Why could Dostoevsky sit without adequate clothing in an unheated room and write *The Brothers Karamazov*? Why are we so soft and tender-skinned today that unless we get our morning cup of coffee, we can't go to business? These are mysteries. It is still a mystery to me why purely physical illness sometimes appears to open avenues for creative work, though at other times it fails." This

shows plainly, he said, that it is dangerous to equate too quickly problems of health, problems of mental and physical disease, with problems of morality and faith.

"The greatest joy of faith and morality ever known by man," he continued, "was that of Saint Francis. You will recall how he passed a leper on the road and experienced a sense of terrific disgust. He felt so bad about it that he turned his donkey around, came back, and with a feeling of nausea and with tears in his eyes, embraced the leper and kissed him, and then went on with a sense of profound joy. It was hardly pleasurable, that experience.

"These are the things of faith that we have not solved, and I think they are the things that we are afraid of."

A clergyman remarked: "I am interested in Dr. Wolff's set of data about the frequency of illness apparent within a relatively minor group. It seems to me there are probably some data that raise questions concerning the relevance of the individual to the particular environment that he identifies himself with, or to his ability to make an adaptation.

"When you look at some of the available data about people who are victims of accidents, or at the data regarding inhabitants of prisons, and the repetitiveness of behavior, both purposeful and accidental supposedly, whereby one maintains a residence in one of these institutions, it seems to me that all of these raise a basic question about what particular world the individual is attempting to maintain himself in, and also a question about whether or not those who are in the majority group are not imposing their own definition of the world that they would like these inmates to live in.

"I notice, for example, among some of my clergy friends a tendency to make certain kinds of judgments about individuals who find no means, apparently, for affiliation with or participation in or service by a religious practitioner or institution.

"If we think of ourselves as being practitioners in the various areas of psychiatry, religion, business, and so forth, each of us has a position within his area and apparently has made a kind of adaptation. There are individuals who do not come within our purview and who are not disciplined by voluntary or involuntary means. Now, it seems to me that to get at this type of person and make him a better individual, whether we mean a more

healthy person, a religious person, or an economically productive person, we deal with a dimension that is often difficult for us to perceive. Were there an anthropologist in our midst, perhaps we could ask him whether or not interpretation, understanding, and even aiding in adaptation and selection of environment to which one is going to adapt rest upon a common thesis that the individual's definition of his environment, the way in which he seeks his goal, the kind of adaptation he makes to the environment of his choice, or the lack of ability to adapt to environment, create a basic problem that we are concerned with here."

Dr. Wolff agreed that it was a problem of concern. "I would say that ideally we should aim to create an atmosphere in which the person's creative gifts lie. I would hope that what we do as teachers and pastors would be to make this the problem of the individual so that he could, by all the devices discovered by man, find out where he fits, what kind of person he is, and what he needs to accomplish his ends."

The previous speaker assented, but pressed for further elucidation. "As practitioners in any of these areas, it seems to me we would have considerable difficulty in discovering what the individual's basic goal is, or substituting a different goal. It is here that we get into trouble as practitioners, and it occurs to me that we sometimes think that the way in which an individual might make a better adaptation, from our reading of things, is to have a substitution of a more satisfactory goal. This is a little more difficult to accomplish, and that is why I am interested in the data you present. How are you going to get these individuals, if goal orientation is a group problem, to substitute the kind of goal orientation, or to clarify a different one, that will change the category of sickness or healthiness that they display in their attempts at adaptation?"

Dr. Wolff replied that, putting it over simply, the individual could learn what his goal should be through the educational process. He added that every therapy, every teaching, every constructive interpersonal relationship was based on the premise that the relationship would enable the persons concerned to learn their own dimensions, and by that knowledge to be energized to pursue their goals.

Another discussant, a clergyman, set goal orientation in a religious frame of reference. "I think we all want to identify

religion and religious living with mental health. One of our central interests in this conference has been precisely the relationship between these two things. Consequently, I thought that the question, 'Is there a relationship between people in total good health and religion?' was an excellent one.

"Now, your answer is: no very discernible relationship—which I accept. I try to say to myself, 'I can see why,' because I think that this is a personal problem. We touched on that, too, and I think there the critical question is, 'To what extent does the individual manage to live up to the ideals and goals that are offered by his religion?' It seems to me that if he does not succeed in doing this, his religion can actually present a problem for him from a mental health point of view, and I think that here psychiatrists should say, 'I think so. This is true.'

"On the other hand, I believe that religion does offer goals that are extremely valuable and helpful to a great many people—for those who can measure up to them. Certainly from my point of view, it is very clear that the Catholic religion is no sinecure. It doesn't make life easy. It makes many things difficult. But if I as an individual am able to measure up to those goals, this is a very powerful support, a great contribution to mental health. This, as I say, is a personal problem.

"A very important thing, it seems to me, is this: the mental health man has to see from a purely mental health point of view that the individual does live up to his own goals. If he does not, he is in conflict and difficulty. But I think religion comes along to suggest a higher goal. This is a forward-going kind of thing. In other words, I see the function of mental health work as trying to help the person live up to his goals and that of religion as helping to give him better goals to strive for."

In answer to a query based on his remark about brain damage resulting from prolonged inappropriate adaptive devices—a question as to whether both psychotherapy and religion may prove ineffective in helping severely damaged persons, such as the schizophrenic, for example—Dr. Wolff said that though there are always end points from which there is no return, he believed that in most cases the process can be reversed and that in the future even more would be done in this direction.

Another member of the group said that he had recently delivered a paper that dealt with the point under discussion. "I began," he said, "by asking whether it is true, as is sometimes alleged, that religion causes insanity. This is something we often hear suggested, but it is also frequently suggested that the reverse assumption is more nearly correct, that religion is conducive to mental health. I think we ought somehow to come to grips with these two opposing views, if we can, and see what truth lies in each of them. I would like to read a brief section of the paper.

" 'It was hailed as a great advance when we began, a century or so ago, to think of the insane as sick rather than sinful, but the gain has been a doubtful one. If a person has sinned, there is always the possibility of repentance and redemption, but if a person is sick, mentally and emotionally sick, what then does he do? Since the illness is not his fault, nor is it within his power to correct, he must turn to others for treatment—treatment which is likely either to be unavailable or prohibitively expensive.' "

The speaker referred to the Old Testament description of Nebuchadnezzar's madness and Daniel's treatment of it. He then read the conclusion of his paper: " 'Religion in its most vital and significant form has always been intent upon saving souls in the sense of helping individuals regain their sense of peace and freedom through a return to responsible living, integrity, and concern and compassion for others.'

"This," he continued, "is therapy of the most profound variety, and it is a great pity that this conception is today accepted in practice with so little confidence.

"Freud's theory was based on the pleasure principle: when pleasure or the pursuit of pleasure, bodily pleasure or organic pleasure, was interfered with, then one became ill.

"The Old Testament conception of illness and the Christian conception of illness, and I think the conception of illness that Dr. Wolff presented, imply that a person becomes ill when his capacity for joy, for harmony, for relatedness, for affiliation, is interfered with and blocked. I think we have been on a forlorn track in looking for the sources of mental illness in the interruption of organic pleasure and sensual pleasure instead of in disruptions in this other sphere."

"Is it proper," asked another participant, "or is it perhaps even presumptuous, to use the scientific approach to problems of spiritual values or problems of the soul? It was suggested yesterday that perhaps it was presumptuous to do so, that these are in an entirely different category; and if this is so, perhaps the conference might disband. I would like to answer this in the positive sense on two scores.

"Man is the only instrument we have with which to study anything. Any other technical instrument is only an extension of man. Therefore, it seems to me that it is essential that we learn everything we can about man the instrument—and this is the responsibility of all sciences, including the social sciences.

"But even further, man is also the organism that seeks and exhibits spiritual values; and since these are manifest only in man and sought by man, it seems to me again that it is the responsibility of the sciences to teach us everything they can about man the exhibitor and seeker, and that this information will be of importance to our religious leaders, because they also need to understand man both as the instrument and as the exhibitor and seeker."

A clergyman in the group recorded himself as happy because he felt the group was getting together, that an accord had been established. He pointed out that successful adaptation involves a certain kind of loss. "Insight involves a kind of losing of your life to save it. When you solve a problem insightfully, you give up the immediate rewards, whatever they are, of the neurosis, or the immediate thing, for a much longer-time kind of goal, which in the end is a much better goal."

One of the laymen present remarked that he thought there was a good deal of semantic confusion in the discussion, and that this prevented the members of the symposium from attacking the problems directly. Another layman felt that progress had been made, and that all were beginning to use a common language.

THE JOINT ROLE OF RELIGION,

BEHAVIORAL SCIENCES, AND MEDICINE

CHAIRMAN
The Rev. Samuel W. Blizzard, PH.D.

DISCUSSION LEADERS
The Rev. Hans Hofmann, PH.D.

The Rev. Noël Mailloux, O.P.

Rabbi Albert A. Goldman

THE JOINT ROLE OF RELIGION,

BEHAVIORAL SCIENCES, AND MEDICINE

INTRODUCTION BY CHAIRMAN BLIZZARD

We have come to the point foreseen by the Committee on Arrangements as the time when certain divergent points of view may be expressed more fully. Our three leaders this afternoon represent three different religious traditions. In view of the thinking expressed, and perhaps what was not expressed, in our preceding meetings, it will probably be helpful to us to have them make more formal statements of their views. We want to have as much interaction as possible in this session. During the presentations of the three statements, if anyone wants to hand me a note about some particular question he wishes especially to have brought up for discussion, I think it will be quite within the rules of the game.

PRESENTATION BY DR. HOFMANN

It is significant that the problem of mental health, with its vague, all-embracing, and intensely personalistic overtones, is so much a focus of public attention today. It may also surprise us that religion is currently so often associated with mental well-being.

Throughout history, man has always had the need to orientate himself in his world, but the necessity for him to achieve a balance between his personal self-realization and his contact with his environment has seldom been more pronounced than it is at present. The contemporary generation, faced with new physical dimensions, grave interpersonal difficulties at home and abroad, and, with all of this, the inability to find meaning in life, is beginning to recognize its insecurity. The source of this insecurity is the failure of our expectations of fulfilling man's needs and solving his human predicament.

What I call scientism, or the evolutionary illusion, is one expectation that has deluded modern man into believing that merely through his scientific discoveries and technological advances he could eradicate all his difficulties and re-create the world and the people in it into a close approximation of his ideal of the way things should be. By collecting more pragmatic, objective data in the fields of the natural, behavioral, and social sciences, he would arrive at and be secure in the absolute truth.

This did not appear to be a totally fantastic expectation when new discoveries in science at first opened man's eyes to countless means of achieving his potentialities. But today we pause to ask, in spite of the fact that the possibilities of science have only been scratched, if man really knows where he is going with all the new scientific knowledge that is enabling him to alter his life outwardly but that is failing to give it any complete motivation, orientation, and inner meaning.

A second hope that has disappointed this generation is the belief that, by adhering to the dogmatism, liturgy, and moralism of traditional religion, we will produce men who are really human and will thus be able to build a new world full of better people. Traditional religion also relies on mysticism to bring about man's fulfillment, and refuses to accept the necessity for man to investigate himself and his environment objectively. Like scientism, traditional religion claims to have in itself the final answer for man.

Our generation also mistakenly believed that higher standards of living and economic abundance would satisfy all its needs. With his material wants taken care of, man would no longer be against man, and all men could lead a fruitful life together. But although we have managed to acquire great material wealth, our interpersonal relationships on every level remain unhealthy. We are unable to face ourselves, to face others, and to accept ourselves and others as individuals who can and should openly relate.

The problem of mental health is the most sensitive indicator of man's inability to orientate himself in his world today. As it has been negatively derived from observation in psychopathology and the behavioral and social sciences, the definition of mental health is human self-awareness in the co-ordination of the somatic, emotional, and rational facets of its existence; while the self experiences itself as separate and different from its environment, it responds to and cofunctions with it as an active particle of the given time and place. This self-awareness both depends upon and affects man's value structure of life, which is the area usually assigned to religion.

In the search for a solution to man's present lack of orientation, religion and science must work together and each must be ready to accept new insights from the other. Science can be an invaluable aid in determining more exactly the effects of religion upon the personality, and can thus help clarify to what extent religion either is detrimental or beneficial to mental health. But it is necessary to emphasize that science can only arrive at an objective relative description in its investigation of religious experiences. It cannot and should not want to attempt to reveal more than reflections on something that may be real but that is only at our disposition phenomenologically. If we are right in our presupposition that religion is something that comes from beyond man and that, therefore, can never be fully grasped by man's finite, human reason, we must accept the fact that it eludes accurate definition. Religion is each individual's conception of and relation to what he knows as the Divine. Because it is unique and personal, it defies categorization.

If science and religion attempt to give meaning in themselves, they have closed themselves to new knowledge by claiming possession of the absolute truth. This is most likely to occur whenever man shuts himself off from fresh insights because he senses that the security of the fort of old beliefs he has built around himself is being threatened. The two main threats to traditional beliefs today are science and technology, which are opening up better means of investigation and are offering more complete understanding, but at the same time are unfolding more space and more mystery than the human mind dares to cope with. Recent developments in psychology and psychotherapy have caused the same danger signal to arise in the realm of the human personality. A vital question is whether religion now will likewise become rigid or will be willing to accept new experiences and new understanding.

Human self-awareness can be developed only if man steps out of himself in order to fully experience what life has to offer and in order to express himself in his world. To experience and to express are specifically human characteristics, very similar to inhaling and exhaling. To be able to experience, or inhale, we must have the confidence to leave ourselves open to new occurrences and to new scientific investigations of them. Man's exhaling is his expression of himself, the imprint he makes on his environment. He cannot be fully human unless he has the self-assurance and freedom to realize himself through the expression of his own unique personality and his singular universal meaning.

While the value of science to man in his experiencing and expressing is unquestionable, the scientific approach should never be used as the shield behind which mediocre scholarship tries to hide its effort to level out all creative differences into an oppressive tyranny. Once such a pretense is permitted, any possibility for the expression and the vital exchange of new creative insights has been forfeited.

If we agree that experiencing and expressing are prerequisites of man's fulfillment, it follows that responsibility is also a condition of being human. Responsibility is man's ability to respond to his environment with the confidence to participate in it. His response should be both scientific and religious, but should be related to the individual lest it become a dead discipline isolated from the realities of human existence. It must also be open enough to make room for the manifestation of every unique human being.

Both science and religion have their different forms of irresponsibility. Science may supply the methods, but it is irresponsible in its neutrality and indifference toward the results it achieves. Religion likewise is irresponsible in claiming that it is an exclusively irrational mystery incapable of being understood by human reason through objective exploration. In its belief that the Divine will magically answer all man's needs, it refuses to recognize the necessity for a better understanding of human nature, and also is blind to the fact that God works through human and mundane means.

It is because of man's difficulty in relating himself realistically to his environment that he falls into the temptation of using his reason to construct a system of logical laws that seem to be sure footholds promising a safe journey over the ground of his lack of orientation. At this point, mental health becomes primarily a religious problem in terms of the human mandate to be constantly concerned with the growing discovery of an ultimate meaning. If man perseveres in a sensitive, questioning search for such a meaning, he will refrain from turning anything he knows or has into a divinely ordained authority that can forever stand on its own. Only through such open-mindedness can we be truly scientific in developing a realistic approach to life and in seeing things in their proper proportion.

Religion deals with man in a very specific way, since it gives him a confidence that he cannot produce on his own and that he doesn't fully find in his environment. It has a double aspect, on the one hand relating man to his God and on the other to the world around him. The special kind of confidence found through religion stems from the fact that man feels he is loved and accepted from beyond himself. Because he is first loved, undeserving as he may be, man is enabled to respond with love and thus becomes the instrument through which the creative power of love is expressed in the world. Released by love from the restricting bonds of fear, he faces his environment with eagerness to participate in the wonders life has to offer.

This love also engenders within the individual a healthy love of self and a self-respect that are essential for a critical evaluation of self without fear. Through an objective understanding of himself, man can achieve a change and growth that will allow him to more adequately realize his potentialities.

If man accepts himself and acknowledges his own worth as an individual, he is no longer afraid of being rejected by others. Once he has been set free by love, he ceases to be self-centered and selfish, but finds it necessary to express this love in interpersonal relationships. He becomes able to accept others as persons also having their own special worth despite their failings, which he has learned to forgive. When individuals feel free to express their own uniqueness and to relate to others in honesty without fear of rejection, both isolationism and collectivism will cease to menace us as they do today.

The love found through religion also gives man one of the most powerful, and certainly the most creative, forces of motivation. Man acts in love not through duty or necessity, but through the joy of creating in his work and of giving of his love to his fellow man. After love has touched man, life holds an entirely new meaning for him.

In its double aspect, religion has two functions of orientating man in his world. First of all, it generates within the individual the self-confidence produced by his relationship to his God, and secondly, it enables man to view his environment with confidence. Unfortunately both of these forms of confidence procreated by religion can be corrupted and misused.

While the self-confidence stemming from religion has the benefits we have already discussed, there is always the danger that it may be perverted into a false sense of security by erroneous religious attitudes. If God is regarded as an indulgent father and the Church as a protective home, man feels so self-contained that he loses all desire to step out and be sensitive to the influences of his environment that permit him to grow. The drugging effect of religious routine will also prohibit a constant development and change in the individual personality. When this perverse result of religion occurs in the individual, the normal development of the religious community is likewise arrested and turned into a self-contented, collectivistic, authoritarian system.

Through the religious belief that the world is God's handiwork, the expression of God's being and intention, man can be certain that nothing in his environment exists for the specific purpose of destroying him. Looking upon the world confidently, he is enabled to go forth and discover. Life beyond the immediate circle of his church and home no longer appears to be a strange and threatening place, a place where he will be forced to prove himself on his own. Because the world has already been given by God, man can explore it without being afraid that he will lose himself in it.

On the other hand, a false sense of confidence in the world will mean that man will be seduced into identifying God and ultimate meaning with his own specific insights on and understanding of reality. In maintaining that his truth is the whole truth, man constructs a religion of his own that has little validity because of its individualistic, legalistic, or moralistic nature.

A religious attitude toward the world can also bear the danger of causing man to lose his orientation completely. If he stops with the conviction that the world is God-created and does not inquire further into the matter, he is liable to have considerable difficulty in co-ordinating this belief with the realities and problems of the human situation. The result here usually is that neither the world nor his place in it makes any sense to him; therefore, he grows indifferent to what occurs around him, loses all desire to find any meaning, and finally becomes pragmatic and opportunistic.

Man manifests the twofold aspect of religion through religious symbols, which are expressions of his relationship to his God, and through the organization of specific religious communities, which express the communal life of religion in the world. But it is most important that neither the symbolic nor organizational side of religion be overemphasized. If the symbolic, which should attempt to be nothing more than a concrete expression of our limited understanding of God, becomes identical with God Himself, we have a rigid, authoritarian religion that leaves no room for the possibilities of new revelation. Religious symbols and liturgy have definite value as manifestations of an inner awareness, but they should never be allowed to become a substitute for it. We are equally in error if we permit any religious organization to claim possession of the absolute truth, and thereby build a tyranny that causes immense confusion and emotional distress. It was exactly these circumstances that prompted the Reformation, a necessary and vital break from the oppression of the past.

We are not denying that the achievements of the past were relevant and constructive within their particular historical context. Nevertheless, we need contemporary courage to evaluate the past in light of the present in order to discern how we can deal with the newness and difference of the future. We must leave the past when it no longer enables us to envision adequately the prospects of the future and to accept new concepts and outlooks.

Finally, religion offers us the freedom to give and take of the fullness of life. It teaches us to be open because we feel sure that there is some fulfillment even though we can't be certain of the exact form it will take. Such openness will permit us to experience a constant rebirth from a previous narrow and distorted self-understanding to a deeper realization of the ultimate meaning of the cosmos and of our unique participation in it. We must develop an attitude like that of a child who can grow because he can always be surprised. Revelation is not grounded once and for all in one historical incident; nor is it a static investment in the laws of nature. It is instead the dynamic, personal, and unique discovery of cosmic meaning in the concrete reality of our human situation.

However, man is seldom very eager to involve himself in the human predicament, so he uses two kinds of escape mechanism to insure himself against the risks he might incur in such an involvement. In order to stay on the safe, easy road he either becomes an experimentalist or an idealist. The experimentalist becomes so immersed in his production of scientific definitions that he ceases to care when his work no longer pertains to life. With his objective formulas, he keeps clear of all entanglements.

The idealist avoids involvement by a different method. In contrast to the objective scientist, he is so subjective that his principles and speculations on life also fail to express reality and point out new avenues on which action can proceed.

In order not to fall into either of these traps, we are attempting to find a way in between them. What we propose to do at Harvard is to establish an inter-discipline study in collaboration with the Harvard Medical Center. With its clinical facilities, the medical center will be the place for carrying on a study of people who, because they are faced with a crisis, manifest the necessity of struggling to find meaning in life, and in doing this, also exemplify the irrelevance of many of our traditional tenets and religious habits. In close co-operation with surgeons, internists, and psychiatrists, highly gifted graduate students of theology will observe at first hand the changes that take place in the religious self-awareness of the patient. They will be trained and aided in this work by competent instructors in psychology and sociology. Professors Allport, McClelland, and Parsons will assure the high quality of such investigation, and the names of Sturgis and Solomon in the field of medicine guarantee the high medical quality of the undertaking.

This project will be carried out over a period of three years. It promises not only to provide material of value to medical education and the social and behavioral sciences, but especially to furnish solid indications of the effects of religion with which all theologians and prospective ministers must concern themselves. Thereby theology and the ministry should be helped to understand realistically what constitutes faith and how it is best developed and challenged.

As other graduate schools have already shifted the emphasis of their study from academic content to the human personality, it is our hope that the schools of theology will gradually follow suit. When using this new approach, theology should ask what, from the great treasure of biblical insights, historical and traditional experiences, doctrinal reflections, and liturgical expressions, comes alive in our human situation today, and hence manifests the dynamic vitality and constant newness of religious experience and faith.

What we really hope for is to produce in a Socratic fashion men and women who are naturally curious enough to integrate a fund of knowledge without either being lost in it or making it their selfish possession. It is our personal prerogative and our responsibility to coming generations to provide, if we can, an opportunity for the scientist to be open to the possibility that the universal may reveal itself in the scientific realm, and for the religious believer to rejoice that his faith becomes more relevant in the midst of scientific investigation directed toward a more honest, mature, and free humanity.

DISCUSSION

At the beginning of the session, a clergyman in the group had posed a question that he hoped might be considered in the discussion period. Assuming that all those present spoke from a common ethos, a common civilization, a common reservoir of ideas that might be labeled the Judaeo-Christian tradition, he took it for granted there would be little disagreement about the definition of a healthy society and a healthy person. What, then, about mental health as adaptation? "Is a person mentally healthy if he adapts well to a sick society? Or is the mentally or spiritually healthy person one who is almost out of joint with much that happens in the society of which he is a part?"

When Dr. Hofmann had finished his presentation, a participant observed that he had made a general statement of what he thought should be a continuing quest for new ideas, but had not said what that had to do with mental health.

Dr. Hofmann said he found it hard to make sense when using such vague terms as "religion" and "mental health." "Religion is an abstraction that has no reality value as such. All you can say is that you, for yourself, have a relationship to God that in turn is related to, and meaningful in, your given feeling of reality, and you may have an explanation for this that is very helpful. For the second point, I think I would rather ask the medical authorities and the psychiatrists among us to tell me first exactly what mental health is. As far as I can see, with my limited insight into the field, all that we can ask for is that there may be an appropriate balance between the individual and his environment, the society, and that this balance in itself may enable the individual to be creative and the environment to be appropriately conservative."

Another member of the group said he agreed with what Dr. Hofmann had said to the effect that finding better means of self-realization would contribute to better mental health, but he asked Dr. Hofmann if he could be more specific about the means of self-realization through the use of religion.

Dr. Hofmann pointed out that he had not suggested that there was a single means of self-realization based on religion, and that the religious needs for self-realization were not the same for everybody. The questioner assented, and said that he thought psychiatry and psychoanalysis had postulated certain things that could help the theologian in his attempt to guide people into utilizing their potentials as fully as possible.

"Mental health in the framework that we have been discussing," said a medical educator in the group, "would be the expression of an individual who succeeds best in finding the part that he is going to play in life, and playing it in a way that is consistent with the production of the best that is in him. Therefore, he has got to have morality to become part of a system larger than himself. This is the evolving social system of which man is a part. His hope is here, his morality is here, and this is his salvation."

Dr. Hofmann referred to the question asked at the opening of the session about the relation of the individual to society. "It may well be," he said, "that we have emasculated true religious insight and potency to make religion merely serve to produce good citizens who divinely glorify the *status quo*. I would, therefore, keep open the possibility that a true religious insight and a truly humble and obedient religious person may run against everything that we like to think is true."

PRESENTATION BY FATHER MAILLOUX

According to the program, I am supposed to present *the* Catholic point of view on this particularly ticklish problem, whose adequate solution still appears to be considerably remote, namely: "The Joint Role of Religion, Behavioral Sciences and Medicine in Regard to Mental Health." More modestly, I merely claim to be allowed to make an improvised attempt at expressing *a* Catholic point of view on this matter. Simultaneously, I will make a very conscious effort to treat this topic in the light of our earlier discussion and of the various considerations that have already been suggested.

Within this frame of reference, two preliminary remarks seem necessary for a clear understanding of the basic positions I intend to assume.

As you will remember, our attention has been repeatedly drawn to the implications of the scientific approach as compared to those of the moral and/or the religious approach to the study of human behavior. Here, undoubtedly, a major source of confusion is our present concept of "science," whose imperialistic pretentions now begin to be more and more challenged. Such pretentions, indeed, are of relatively recent origin, but they frequently induce us to forget that this concept of science is limited in scope. Essentially operational in nature, the scientific concept had already appeared for centuries as particularly appropriate to tackle the disconcerting variability of the most contingent aspects of natural phenomena, although it could not be applied effectively for a long time because of the lack of mathematical insights and of measurement devices. On the other hand, the traditional concept of "natural science" extends far beyond the description of phenomena in terms of quantitative scales, comparative-frequency ranking, significant correlations, and conjectural predictability. Whatever general laws are formulated on the basis of these raw data, they merely express some operational or pragmatic interrelations and, at most, open the way for new technological applications. But we cannot be satisfied with learning how to make the best possible use of natural energy. Well-controlled empirical data also provide a fresh point of departure for inductive or deductive insights, which result in more fundamental explanations and entail some integrated causal, structural, dynamic, and teleological interpretations. As we begin to deal with less contingent factors, the spectrum of probability may be so reduced that, even on the basis of a single observation or experiment, some actually meaningful conclusion can be immediately reached instead of some blind mathematical approximation.

Perhaps this confusing reductionism is just a more deeply rooted and more persistent manifestation of a rather naïve bias that has been surreptitiously creeping into the field of psychological research. This, however, should be denounced all the same, and should be eradicated if the kind of synthesis that we are now contemplating is to be effectively achieved. Since the days when Wundt attempted to build up a "psychology without a soul," not because he denied the reality of the soul but for the sake of testing his new experimental methodology, we have been constantly confronted with the equivocal tendency to identify the whole psychological science with the one method or theory that happened to be the fashion of the moment. Thus, one after the other, we witnessed the sweeping invasions of Pavlovian reflexology, of behaviorism, of *Gestalt* theory, and, finally, of psychoanalysis, all displaying the same uncompromising and tightly impervious claims. It was only too understandable, then, that we tended to forget that the total scope of a science is determined by its subject-matter, and not by any particular object falling within its sphere whose consideration may call for a different methodological approach. After all, why should we be less versatile than the sculptor, who will modify his techniques whenever he chooses to work with wood rather than marble, or with plaster rather than bronze, but will nevertheless continue to regard whatever he is accomplishing as falling within the realm of sculpture?

No wonder, then, if empirical science relies on statistical methods when it attempts to cope with the relative probability governing the apparently diffuse variability of human behavior, while it prefers inductive-deductive methods when it tries to elucidate its structural and dynamic determinants, or resorts to some sharp intuitive methods when it looks for its deepest and most intricate motivations. As you will remember, the violent opposition that Freud met in the academic world was not provoked by his hypotheses relative to psychosexual development, as he himself seemed to think, along with certain of his followers. Anyone who studied at any of the better-known American universities during the 1930's can easily recall that what then appeared to be particularly upsetting was, first, Freud's attempt to offer a causal interpretation of behavior that boldly made use of a specifically mental energy; and, second, his attempt to offer an explanatory interpretation of behavior that, through the principles of psychic determinism and of overdetermination, led to the reintroducing of teleology.

In the light of this broader consideration, it becomes clear that the dialogue between religion and the behavioral sciences must inevitably be resumed. Indeed, Freud's twofold interpretation is, on one hand, forcing on us a developmental and dynamic concept of psychic functioning that involves a thorough study of the concrete relationship existing between phantasy and reason, instinctual impulses and free will; and, on the other hand, while heading at the deep motivations of human behavior, is raising the problem of ultimate as well as of immediate goals and values.

The theologian is dealing with the concept of a spiritual and immortal *soul,* not at all coinciding with our empirical concept of the *psyche,* which the theologian calls *sensualitas.* From his viewpoint, although the soul is endowed with all the biological energies, potentialities and functions of the psyche, it is not radically swayed by the mere attraction of pleasure, which is spontaneously, albeit with painful inconsistency, superseded by the attraction of joy, and transcending universal happiness as soon as the prevailing of reason and will induces the dawn of spiritual pursuits. To the theologian, also, all the forces of aggression appear to be ultimately in the service of love—that is, of *caritas,* whose highest expression consists in an overwhelming and disinterested attachment to God. In Him, indeed, the theologian discovers at the same time the infinite good and the fulfillment of our cravings for a long-awaited happiness which needs to be conquered through the most strenuous efforts and constant struggling against the forces of evil. Therefore, beyond the pleasure principle, the theologian is tracing something far more positive than the primacy of the death instinct, and he will unremittingly take exception to the assertion that "the goal of all life is death."

While looking at man, the theologian considers the unfolding of his fundamental inclinations in the light of his essential structure, insofar as these inclinations allow man to elucidate his universal orientation and his most successful individual expressions. Therefrom, the theologian derives an insight leading to the grasping of *natural law* together with the goals and values that are ingrained in our spontaneous aspirations. This will, as it were, supply the necessary basis for the progressive formulation of the norms that are expected to regulate the rational adaptation of our individual behavior to unique conditions of living.

As to the scientist, he is equally preoccupied with that kind of structural and existential approach. However, to put it again in the words of the theologian, he is not interested in our actions as they are typically *human*—that is, as elicited under the direction of a deliberate free will, but simply as they are the *actions of man.* Knowing from observational data that human nature is not always functioning at its best, he is on the lookout, not to define more accurately the specific implications of natural law, but to render explicit the *laws of nature*—that is, the principles underlying the various patterns of mores actually exhibited by individuals, endowed with all the potentialities of human nature, but submitted to the vicissitudes of psychological development and to the pressures of social, educational, and cultural influences.

It is self-evident that the theologian cannot but rely heavily on such empirical information supplied by the behavioral sciences. From time immemorial, he has insisted that while it is imperative to start moral training early in life and to help children and adolescents to develop precocious virtuous habits, no one can possibly acquire a deep insight into the meaning of moral behavior and understand all the intricacies of scientific moral reasoning before he has reached sufficient maturity and has had the time to secure a wide personal experience of human affairs. To build up a normative science, designed to provide our conscience with adequate guidance so that it can cope with the constant turmoil of our inner life and with the ever-changing external situations and circumstances in which it has to pass judgment, one has to become familiar with the complexity of human motivations and capable of making a precise estimation of all facets of reality. This is to say that any bit of scientifically controlled experience will inevitably prove to be of tremendous avail for the developing of moral science.

A great deal more could be said to suggest the kind of illuminating synthesis that might result from an effective searching collaboration between theology and the behavioral sciences. However, both the theologian and the scientist are precluded from remaining in the ivory tower of knowledge, confronted as they are with the very concrete task of helping their fellow men to implement values in their daily life or to preserve their mental equilibrium. Here, again, several problems emerge that require close consideration on both sides. They can be satisfactorily elucidated only through our joint efforts, and their crucial importance appears undeniable to anyone interested in a comprehensive humanistic approach.

In this practical perspective, our immediate goal consists of liberating man from the clouds of infantile prelogical thinking as well as from the fetters of deterministic psychological mechanisms, activated by inwardly mobilized unconscious and unrealistic conflicts. It is only when an individual has developed and properly trained his capacity for rational free choice that he becomes able to display self-control in his ordinary behavior and to replace thoughtless conformity by insightful, virtuous self-regulation. Whether we have the opportunity of observing at close range those who succeed in achieving such a high degree of moral maturity or those who fail even to pass the threshold of freedom, we all feel some dire shortcomings as soon as we attempt to grasp the whole developing process of personality, with all its crises and growing pains, its integrative potentialities, and creative innovations. Only an exchange of experience would allow such basic insights shared by the members of each group to reach usefully across the lines that separate our disciplines, if the barriers to communication can finally be broken down.

The next crossroad where we probably could compare notes and give a great deal of help to one another is supplied by the inevitable interference of a superego, implanted from without, with our moral conscience, which progressively comes to express the demands of an autonomous reason. Certainly, the highly disinterested motives that dictate our most mature moral decisions have nothing in common with the narcissistic ones that at first incite each of us to turn away from evil and follow the right path. The former may even be desperately conflicting with the latter, as it only too often happens with the greatest saints, who rarely reach the fulfillment of their inner spiritual aspirations and the heights of their contemplated accomplishments without knowing the throes of dire frustrations, of general disapproval, and even of hateful rejection. Inevitably, then, while they obey their conscience, they have to struggle with the depressing reprobation of a latent, but often unexpectedly cruel, superego. And here, perhaps, it is necessary to draw attention to the fact that the interference of a reactivated superego does not merely involve the well-known threat of subtle bribery and of unconscious contamination of noble motivations through some disguised narcissistic wishes. It also entails a rather peculiar type of distorted guilt reaction, which has been barely noticed and is still awaiting careful and penetrating scrutiny. As long as it is one's moral conscience that passes judgment on sinful behavior, the individual will see clearly that he has *done* the wrong thing and, as does everyone who recognizes an error, he will immediately grasp why and how he should change his course of action. Moreover, if he begins to feel sincere regret for what he has done, he will entertain no anxiety about the possibility of receiving the pardon of God and men.

Now, should a neurotic superego enter into the picture, we immediately notice that the individual no longer passes judgment on his actions but on himself. He will insist that he *is* intrinsically worthless, and will show little or no insight as to the possibility of straightening out his usual ways of behaving. Also, the expectation of being forgiven will tend to wane completely, unless some miraculous opportunity be offered to undo the evil once committed and to start all over again. Needless to say, this basic change of attitude is of such importance as to require an exhaustive study on the part of all of us.

But we cannot engage in the aforementioned investigations without soon feeling compelled to raise another question, which may have a tremendous impact on our attempted interpretations. The theologian has always regarded human conduct practiced for the mere sake of sensual satisfaction as disorderly and sinful. Nowadays, the psychologist goes one step further and does not hesitate to say that such behavior will soon become disturbed. The latter, indeed, looks at some ego function as to a function that is served in the performance of realistic and useful purposes by well-domesticated instinctual energy. This means that it has been purified from an overinvestment of libidinal energy, or that it has been delibidinized to the point where there will be no more risk that it be deflected from the pursuance of its prescribed aims by the attraction of pleasure. Normally, its exercise will continue to involve a fair share of satisfaction, but this secondary aim will remain subordinate to the more rational aims sought by the ego, thus rendering their attainment much easier.

Usually, this displacement of psychic energy in the direction of socially approved aims takes place unconsciously, under the pressure of education. It is called sublimation. In turn, the theologian suggests that if sensuality succeeds in creeping into the realm of reason and in deviating some of its functions in the direction of purely hedonistic aims, the reverse seems also true. But here the theologian is not satisfied with the mechanical process of sublimation. His experience with asceticism has made him aware that as a consequence of deliberate virtuous control, sensuality may undergo deep intrinsic transformations instead of mere quantitative and directional displacements. By being repeatedly instrumental in rational and moral achievements, sensuality becomes truly imbued with spiritual dynamism and, acquiring the inexhaustible versatility of intellectual intuition and reasoning as well as of voluntary decision, it supplies the fertile soil for imaginative insights and for energetic initiatives. This ascending process, far exceeding the limits of precarious sublimations, virtually raises sensuality to a level of ecstatic efficiency that sometimes leads to unexpected creativeness. Yet, although it has been given casual attention, it awaits systematic empirical inquiry.

Finally, among the numerous other problems that should be mentioned in this initial presentation, let us choose the one that has already come to the fore and undoubtedly deserves more penetrating consideration. If we want to understand each other more adequately, it is necessary for the psychologist, who speaks of object love, to become clearly aware at least of the attitudinal dispositions implied in the theologian's broader concept of *caritas,* not to speak of its other transcending components. How can we forget that Freud himself, who regarded the capacity for object love as the very criterion of sound psychological equilibrium, found it impossible for man to love his enemies? This is an indication that our clinical approach to the problem of object love is merely tackling the functional aspect of such interpersonal relationship—that is, the chief aspect an empirical scientist will feel spontaneously inclined to be interested in. The alternative of object love consists in an infantile narcissistic pattern of emotional functioning, which leaves us incapable of perceiving others as autonomous beings, equally entitled as we are to have ideals, goals and wishes of their own, and locks us up in an egocentric attitude, totally impervious to their most legitimate expectations. This merely implies that one who has reached the level of object love can display the sort of elementary disinterestedness that will make it possible for him to express respectful altruistic consideration for others. This is certainly a great deal; but it is not all. For example, such an individual may renounce the attempt to seduce another person, although he continues to entertain such a desire, because this other person refuses to yield to his advances for moral reasons. He can be said to be fully respectful of others' feelings, to have surmounted his narcissistic or egocentric impulses, to be capable of genuine object love; still, on moral grounds, he may remain an unrepenting *egoistic* individual, and the theologian will never think that his way of life is inspired by *caritas*. In other words, *caritas* involves a value element that appears alien to object love unless the latter is totally devoid of sinful selfishness and has assumed the transcendent viewpoint of a theological virtue. It would be of tremendous interest for the psychologist to know more about the deep transformation occurring in our natural dynamism under the *value-creating* influence of theological and moral virtues, since this definitely leads to the improvement of its functioning and, eventually, to unsuspected human achievements.

This last consideration, as it were, is an invitation to center the following concluding remarks on the problem of the so-called role of religion in regard to mental health. From what has already been said, it is clear enough that we have still a long way to go before we can give a satisfactory answer to this vitally important but, at the same time, frightfully complex question. However, certain confusing and rather naïve misconceptions should be disposed of right from the start, if our planned inquiry is to proceed realistically.

On the part of those who intend to make a significant contribution toward the elaboration of a far-reaching synthesis, an earnest effort will be required to secure a clear understanding of the tenets of religion and of their implications for human life. No illuminating conclusions can be expected to emerge from the puerile pragmatic formulations advanced by superficial propagandists and, too often, even by well-intentioned scientists who, in their disquieting disappointment with science's failure to promote human betterment, are timidly turning back to religion with a more benevolent attitude. The issue involved will have to be faced in its whole integrity, and no informed theologian will accept the platitudes proffered by those who feel inclined to make use of religion, as they might do with occupational therapy, because it may bring comfort to the *average man* in occasional distress, and help him to pull himself together by providing the sort of teleological interpretation of his universe that will satisfy his wishful fantasies and infantile needs.

Let us not forget that the core of neurosis lies in some unconscious inner conflict induced by disturbed emotional functioning.

Certainly, when confronted with depressing mental duress, a sincerely religious man may find in himself more courage to endure his prolonged sufferings, and, even in utter despair, his acceptance of moral principles may prevent him from committing suicide. This does not mean, however, that he is acting with genuine rational lucidity. But although his capacity for making a deliberate choice is dangerously impaired, he continues to feel under the spell of deeply ingrained moral habits. In ordinary circumstances, our expectations should not be that his mental condition is going to be straightened out by his religion but, rather, that his religion will also be impaired and unwillingly distorted under the pervasive influence of unfolding neurotic processes.

From our viewpoint, then, it is far more important to recall that religion, insofar as it involves a total dedication to the service of God, is bound to have a tremendous impact on one's way of life. Undoubtedly, its demands will be farther-reaching and more exacting than the ones resulting from the earnest assumption of parental and social responsibilities. Those who have been striving to implement their religious convictions in their daily activity know very well that they cannot escape experiencing disquieting tensions, and that this aspect of personality development has also its many unforeseen vicissitudes. It is to live up to these transcendent aspirations that they will want to get rid of paralyzing neurotic conflicts and to receive the enlightened guidance that may be secured through the combined insights of theological meditation and empirical observation. Inasmuch as the behavioral sciences will help render man capable of utilizing the dynamic resources of his faltering free will more readily and effectively for the attainment of spiritual achievements, they will be of tremendous avail to religion.

Similarly, we can hope that through their thorough study of prelogical thinking, behavioral scientists will provide us with some means to prevent so many individuals from entering on the road of superstitious illusions. It is no easy task, indeed, to keep religious symbolism uncontaminated by distorting magical fantasies, and even scientists are rarely aware of its precise significance. Very few among them pay any attention to the fact that it has been refined and enriched by centuries of rigorous theological reflection. Their all-too-frequent reductionistic interpretations appear simply ludicrous to the theologian, who is fully aware of the intuitive enlightenment resulting from meaningful analogies, and knows how these are stretching our spiritual horizon far beyond the limits of our strictly logical understanding.

Admittedly, such a sketchy presentation will bring little clarification to the problem submitted for discussion. Not a single issue has been exhaustively explored and no solutions have been proposed. However, at this stage, you will kindly recognize that somebody had to be brave enough to indicate some few landmarks for further investigations, and that this initial formulation had to assume the bold appearance of a provocative challenge.

DISCUSSION

The first question was raised by a psychologist. "I was very much interested in Father Mailloux's distinction between a neurotic and a person who sins. The person who sins says, 'I have sinned,' and then can do something about it; the neurotic thinks of himself as, in a sense, condemned, bad, weak entirely. But isn't it possible also for a sinner to say of himself, 'I am a sinner,' and to have just as hopeless a feeling as the neurotic has when he thinks of himself as bad? It reminds me of something that Hayakawa said about the difference between the individual who says, 'I have failed three times' and the person who says, 'I am a failure.' Can't the same thing apply to the sinner? Can he say, 'I am a sinner' with the same consequences as in the case of the person who says, 'I am a neurotic'?"

Father Mailloux replied, "Yes, he would say that, but you see, he would say, 'I am a sinner because I have sinned.' The other one is just reversing the situation: 'Look how bad I am!' I think it is a very basic observation. I think with any neurotic there is a tendency to tie the self-esteem with the subject and not with the behavior, because even if I am behaving badly, that doesn't mean that I am bad. I can do much better."

In other words, said the discussant, the sinner can see the possibility of pardon. Father Mailloux added that in the case of the sinner, there was constant observation, but that depressed persons could never admit the possibility of redemption or salvation or forgiveness.

The psychologist surmised that there could be a combination of the two attitudes. "You could have somebody who thinks he has sinned and then becomes neurotic in the sense that he feels 'I have sinned' or 'I am a sinner' to such a degree that he says 'I cannot get redemption.' Would that then be moving over into the neurotic sphere, as you see it?"

Father Mailloux said that the problem was a knotty one. "I think that sometimes when you are in such a position—this has been observed by Saint John of the Cross— it is very difficult to make a distinction as to whether the person is so depressed because he is self-accusing. It means that he may verbalize his feeling of inadequate behavior, or inadequate moral behavior, in such a way that even his neurosis is involved. Such a person feels at the same time that he is bad."

The participant suggested that there was an important distinction between those who accepted responsibility and those who abrogated it. Father Mailloux agreed. "The one will say, 'I have sinned.' That means, 'I am responsible for what I have done, and now I know how to do better.' "

"And the person who says, 'I am bad'?" asked another group member.

Father Mailloux replied, "This is the sort of thing that we observe also. It is very strange that self-accusers, or the ones who are anxious about sin, always reach a point where they don't recognize any responsibility at all."

"What does religion do with the self-accusers, the neurotics?" another participant asked.

"I think the first thing to do," answered Father Mailloux, "is to tell them that they are neurotic, and that they should not look to religion as a means to cure a neurosis. The sacraments are made to give grace and to make you better, but not to cure you of neurosis. God may give you that as a favor. It may be a miracle. It is not impossible, but the sacrament is not specifically meant for that. I think as priests we must make them aware of their sickness right from the beginning."

The questioner asked if it weren't true that ministers and priests failed their parishioners because they hadn't been taught to recognize neuroses as such. Father Mailloux replied that such things as neuroses have only recently been understood by clergymen. The clergy must receive better training.

A Protestant clergyman remarked: "I think the person who

says, 'My behavior is bad' is really suffering remorse, isn't he, Father? He has a generalized sense of guilt."

Father Mailloux rejoined, "Inferiority."

PRESENTATION BY RABBI GOLDMAN

I would like to present this particular viewpoint as one that is essentially my own. It is based on my understanding of the topic as it reflects my approach to it in terms of religious experience that I, as a Jew, can equate with the search for mental health.

At this point, I don't have to define the state of mental health, but rather what I understand it to be and what I derive from Judaism as the common equations and the equivalents of where we are moving in certain directions and where we are not. I shall try to put this under three brief headings, and to say that in these areas I think that my Jewish experience, or at least the culture of Judaism, has been working in this direction.

First, I would say, Judaism is a culture, a religion of civilization that has a sense of creativity. It begins with a pronouncement. We in Judaism are not systematic metaphysicians. Our seeming indifference to metaphysics is explained by the fact that we begin our concepts of life a little bit differently. We begin with the concept of the Bible: *In the beginning, God.* We don't ask what is the nature of God, what is the nature of being; there is here the sense of affirmation; there is here an immediate imprint, if you will, upon reality. And we say that this is a creative universe, a creative, living God, and that creativity is a natural aspect of man and is a necessity in his innate being.

Now, in Judaism we ask, "How do we understand man? What is our approach to man?" In Judaism we have not developed any profound Aristotelian concepts, although we favor them. There was the concept simply that man is always locked in a conflict. He has within him two innate impulses, the good and the evil. The evil is not in itself thoroughly evil, the good in itself is not thoroughly good; but we would classify this as two potentialities.

Man, then, is in this creative tension. He is in this creative tension in which he is constantly becoming. He is in no state of absolutism, but he is a creature who has within himself a creativity to work upon himself, to direct himself and to deal with the material that is innate in him. Thus the creative aspect of Judaism says that the *becomingness* of man is what is so important to us. He is a potential, and it is in the manner in which he acts within his culture as he understands it that his potentiality can be released. Therefore, in Judaism we have not, for example, accepted some other theological concepts such as original sin. We rather see man in original tension. This is his fate. He must direct himself.

The creativity of man, as we understand it, then, is that he must constantly work upon himself, he must handle himself, he must deal with himself. Man is given, however, a tool. We call it the Torah. In this vast literature, in the Bible, and in all of the Jewish heritage, we have said, "This is the way in which a man reaches his full state of manhood, his maturity, his adulthood," or: "The peak of his goal in life is righteousness." This is his goal. Our goal in this sense is that he must be a just, righteous individual. This is what his function, his task in life, is, and it is in this area that he serves creatively. He acts, then, morally. His creativity is a moral conflict, and in the handling of this morality he must know his evil. He must know his sin. He must look deep within himself.

There is a rather pertinent passage in one of our teachings that says to us that when the evil impulse begins to disturb man he must drag it into the House of Study. We of the present day have said, "Drag it to the psychoanalyst's couch and there begin to know it." But what was inferred was that to know self was to gain insight through study. This is the approach that Judaism has creatively taken in this vast concept.

Now, the second point that I think is basic to the Jewish concepts—and I began with creativity because the Jew has a starting point in life—is that he has a goal. He becomes part of what he thinks is a process. This is a process, let us say, of urgency. It is a process in which he says, "There is a reality."

I am not going to refute Dr. Hofmann when he implies that we never know reality. It is true that we don't, but we might say religion or Judaism in particular is a way of acting upon reality. It is the manner in which we assume that reality means something, and we create a system of work in which the individual is worthy. He has his role and he has his place and he is fulfilling the work of creation. It is this, I think, that is so basic to us that we cannot help affirming creation. Here, as in psychological language, we affirm sex because we partake of the nature of creation.

Now, a further contribution that I think Judaism gives us for this kind of approach is that we are a religion of command. It would be very hard if someone were to ask me, "What is the Jewish word for faith?" or "What is the Jewish word for religion?" We actually do not possess a clear-cut word. Judaism is a religion of faith, a culture—any one of the words, and I must use them interchangeably, that say it is the act, it is what we call the *mitzvah,* it is the fulfillment of the deed. Behavior in Judaism is the most important aspect. Therefore, we are not, as such, a religion of metaphysics or even of systematic theology. There is no systematic theology in Judaism, there is simply a concept that the most important aspect is behavior, conduct. It is conduct that counts, so that all of our emphasis and all of our attempt has been to define conduct. How does a man reach the holy? How does he reach the righteous? How does he invest in every act of his life the holy and the righteous? In this sense, "behavioral" is no new term to us; it has been our concept.

People sometimes misunderstand what we in Judaism mean by the word *law.* We don't mean something rigoristic or legalistic. We mean simply how every act of life, from the moment of birth to the moment of death, from the moment of rising to the moment of returning to one's sleep, how every act, whether it be a biological act, a sexual act, a gastronomical act, or a spiritual act, is invested with holiness. The whole concept of Judaism in this sense is, "How do people act? What does the Jew do?" You might say this is Judaism.

Now, in this sense, we would have no particular quarrel as such with the behavioral sciences, providing that the behavioral sciences are willing to affirm the concepts of creativity, of worth, of value, and of goals. Seemingly we have achieved this.

We say in this word "command"—and this may be our tension—that man is always in tension with his world. We call this tension the prophetic. The prophetic simply is what is and what ought to be. It is this willingness or attempt to see life from the values of what we understand by God as the source of righteousness; that it is righteousness that must be invested in life and personality, and that the prophetic is the acting of the divine, the pursuit of righteousness in all acts of man. A man is commanded to this righteousness. It is because of this that he must constantly be in tension. The prophet is *against* in order to be *for*. He must work upon his human materials in order to create the higher standards of justice, of righteousness and morality.

It is at this point that we in religion, perhaps, and more particularly in Judaism, may be in conflict with the behavioral sciences. These do not have such an approach to society, a social dynamism as far as society is concerned or even a social goal, a social philosophy in the sense that man has a movement toward some kind of society in which the values of life and justice must be approximated and must be reached and extended in every area of society.

My own personal difficulty with psychology, then, is very often that it describes social movements, but it has no social philosophy. It has not presented an approach to the problems of life. It may describe the tensions that are at work, but it calls man to no particular action. In religion, whether it be Catholic, Protestant, or Jewish, there is this sense of the urgent demand. We, in religion, are called to an action.

In this sense, then, we say, "This is reality," the reality of the act, the reality of the creative command, or, as is more commonly used, the word "commitment." Man is committed, and this is not simply an act that he creates on the analytic couch. It is part of his nature as a free, responsible human being to express through himself this command that is innately his, to act upon his world, to bring it redemption, to bring it to its higher self.

At this point, it seems to me that we meet at certain empirical levels, but religion here must come with the drive, with the dynamism, with the passion, and with the conviction that all of this is worthy, and if it is worthy it must be used creatively by man.

Another factor that all of us have sensed—and perhaps this might have come in some way through the rise of the psychiatric sciences—is that we have all basically agreed here, whether it be man's isolation or man's alienation, that man simply no longer lives in a community. He is alone. This is the theme of existential literature. He is alone in his dread—and it is sometimes a little hard for me to understand because it is not basically part of my experience, but it seems that this emphasis upon the individual aloneness must perhaps reflect a deeper sickness in our society, and the deeper sickness, it seems to me, is that we have lost the sense of community.

Judaism has always emphasized what Kurt Lewin so well put, that what any society needs and what any group needs is a sense of its shared destiny. It is this, I think, that modern life is seeking but hasn't found. Perhaps in the religious groups there is something of this left, but unless psychology or the psychiatric sciences, which deal with this self of man—man in search of himself —can say, "Here are the ways in which man shares his destiny," or "These are the visions that inspire him to bring himself into relationship with other human beings"—unless it becomes part of his sharing goals and values, and develops into a community of men acting in command, acting creatively upon this commitment and for this community, it seems to me all of our thought will remain meaningless. We must tie it to new goals and new drives and new dynamic hopes for man.

It is this, I think, that we in Judaism have attempted to create in a healthy sense. We are a community, a community that perhaps in this country reflects all of the aloneness and all of the inner tensions and divisiveness and dissensions from which we suffer. But it seems to me that the task of psychiatry, religion, and all of the forces dealing with man—even those we term today as interpersonal—is this attempt to create a new sense of community. It is this that Father Mailloux speaks of as a depersonalization or devaluation of man. The devaluation of modern man has come because he has no sense of community. The religions suffer just as much because they have not created a sense of community, sharing the command and sharing the commitment.

Therefore, from my own experience, there are certain things I want to take out of mental health and inject into religion, and vice versa, and I want to harness those forces that are bringing us mental health or new goals or new guides to create it. We have to think in the larger sense not only of the therapy of the individual, but the world in which he is going to live and the world he must act upon. Psychiatry without the prophetic, as far as I am concerned, does its work up to a level, but without the prophetic it does not place man in the world with any sense of shared destiny or shared goals.

DISCUSSION

"It seems to me," began a psychiatrist in the group, "that I note a great difference in therapies. The therapists who are trying to help people interpret and are successful in it are those who meet this challenge of illness, of destructiveness, with a sense of urgency, of caring, of community. They are the therapists who are able to enter into a community relationship with a patient and who feel that there is something creative possible out of the relationship even with a sick person. With them, therapy is not just an intellectual process—a matter of observation, of trying to make the unconscious conscious—but rather the development of creative human relationships in response to the urgency of illness. I think that we do not often think of the various types of therapists. We are all classifying the types of patients, types of conditions and of society, but there are few studies of the types of therapists."

The chairman asked the discussant if he wanted to distinguish among the various types of therapists. "I haven't classified them except in one sense," he said. "I feel that the therapist who is very cool, aloof, objective, and obsessive with his ritual, as he has been taught to proceed, who doesn't get involved with his patient, is not as good as the one who perhaps hasn't had as good training, or who perhaps is not as brilliant or penetrating, or so perceptive of psychopathology. This latter group is much more effective. I think they are alive to what Rabbi Goldman has described as the social and religious problems. I haven't identified this feeling as religion, and these therapists who feel this way would not speak of themselves as religious; but it seems to me that this distinction is pretty clear over the course of the years."

Another member of the group agreed. "What you have been saying about psychiatrists is exactly the same kind of thing that those of us in the ministry see among our colleagues. The ministers who are understanding and loving and kind and permissive and accepting and non-judgmental, who have a sense of security in their own lives and a basic trust and a certain integrity about the values in which they believe—these are the ones who make the greatest progress with disturbed people."

A physician-teacher added that "the best teacher is not the one who tries to give of his wisdom, but of his lovingness."

"I think that we are all grateful to Rabbi Goldman," said one of the psychologists, "for presenting his point of view and for saying so succinctly and so well some of the things that some of us have felt rather more vaguely. The point has been made here that perhaps the religionists must carefully learn the point beyond which they must not go. I think we need to re-examine this proposition. It seems to mean that religion can deal only with the conscious aspects of personality and should leave the unconscious processes and manifestations to the secular professions."

The discussant then read a pertinent passage from a paper: "Now if the secular professions had scored a great success along these lines, or if religion had no precedent or logical justification for interest in the more profound forms of psychopathology, this attitude would be understandable; but neither of these assumptions is true, and one can only be puzzled, along with Dr. Boyce, as to why the churches build and support hospitals for the physically ill but have disclaimed interest or confidence in the so-called mental diseases. If a man's body were in danger, the church would be ready to minister to him, but if his mind and soul were in dire crisis he would be quietly put away in a state hospital without benefit of clergy.

"Anthropologists tell us that the American Plains Indians commonly used dancing and chanting to treat disorders of the mind and body, and if one asked a group of dancers what they were doing in a case where the victim's difficulties were mainly mental, they would say that his soul had left the tribe and they were trying to bring it back. 'Preposterous nonsense!' we scoff, but at least here was an expression of intense community concern and commitment. Who could hear and see his friends and neighbors dancing and chanting for him for hours, or perhaps days on end, without experiencing a profound determination to do whatever was within his power to effect a reconciliation and recovery?

"If someone in our group were suffering from alienation of spirit, we would speak of it in whispers and would be relieved to have him safely out of the way with a minimum of inconvenience to ourselves."

The speaker continued: "I think Rabbi Goldman has put his finger very squarely on the crux of a central cultural issue in our time. We do not have cultural provisions or institutions for bringing the alienated spirit back to the tribe—or holding it there in the first place—and I think we need new concepts and, indeed, new cultural institutions to re-establish, as Rabbi Goldman said so beautifully, the sense of community and commitment."

"I would like to discuss the question of community in a somewhat more direct and perhaps more limited form," said another psychologist. "I mean the problem of the relationship of the individual to his community in the sense of what many psychologists have called 'belongingness.' I know that this has concerned many religious leaders. To some extent, at least, the notion of belongingness has been put in terms of psychological and mental health. This is the sort of thing one hears: The individual—the Jew or the Catholic, say, and it may hold for certain Protestant groups as well—is alienated from his group if he doesn't have a feeling that he is part of his group. And then things go wrong with him psychologically.

"I want to ask two questions. Can Rabbi Goldman or anybody else tell us what this does to the individual, apart from the observations that some people have made, the anecdotal experiences, and so on? Is there anything that tells us how important that sense of belonging to a particular religious group actually is from the point of view of mental health?

"And secondly, I want to know what is the community that we are talking about here. When we speak of the sense of community, should it be for a Jew the sense of belonging to his Jewish group and for a Catholic the sense of belonging to his Catholic group, or should it be, as some religious leaders and some humanists have argued, that the community must be the whole world—the 'for-whom-the-bell-tolls' idea?

"Then my related question is: to what extent does community —in the sense of the smaller kind of group community—aid or interfere with the feeling of community with the larger group? Now, I realize that that is a complicated problem, but I think it is an important one. From the standpoint of mental health and in terms of relationship to other people, how valuable is it to feel strongly identified with a relatively small group? What are the advantages and disadvantages that this gives in relation to identification with a larger group? Can I, as an individual, identify myself more easily with my Catholic and Protestant colleagues here if I am identified with the Jewish group? Or can I identify myself more easily with them if I am not so closely identified with the Jewish group? I don't know the answers, but I think it is a problem of some importance."

Rabbi Goldman said he didn't know all the answers either. "Recently I met with some individuals of the Mennonite group, and I think that what I learned from them is àpropos to your third question about the small group. The Mennonite group, particularly in my area, the Middle West, is undergoing a breakdown. It is becoming urbanized. These people report that mental illness has increased, and so have delinquency and crime among them. They attribute this to the fact that they have left the farms, they have left the structure of their culture, and now are in another area where adjustment processes have to occur, and they are not succeeding too well at this stage.

"At this point we can say that if their observations are correct, this sense of alienation and breakdown is inducing many problems, religious, individual, and social. Somebody ought to study this group to see what really happens to a group in transition, a group in passage away from itself. I would say that such a group has to face the dangers of its inner disorganization, which must reflect upon the inner disorganization of the self.

"In the same way, when I speak of belongingness, I don't divorce the belonging itself and the authenticity of oneself and one's identification with self from that of one's group. Now, that doesn't mean we draw curtains. I think any creative, mature person lives on various levels and identifies himself with values of various levels. I can identify myself as a Jew, let us say, with democracy. I may identify myself with certain aesthetic values, with certain philosophic values, which may not be innate to my immediate culture; but I have here what I think is, at least for myself and for those who share this with me, an inner sense of security. I have a sense of knowing who I am and what part of myself I think is authentic to my nature, to my experience, to my background. It is not something I particularly care to break with, because it has become meaningful to me and to those around me.

"The minority group is aware of the self-hating aspects of oneself, the feeling of the minority, the sense of isolation, the not being accepted, the difficulties in adjustment in the world. And very often I must ask: is this because of one's culture, or perhaps of one's primary experience, that learning to be a Jew follows learning to hate oneself? I could almost make the equation, I think perhaps correctly, that if one learns to love himself or accept himself, he will accept many of the things about him. If he is an escapist, he can express this in a secondary manner against his culture and against his faith and religion, so that what he is actually doing, in my opinion, is escaping from himself.

"The question of belonging is, therefore, not merely belonging to a group or culture; it is belonging simply to oneself and what one's heritage says: 'This is a human being of value.' From my viewpoint, this is my authenticity. This is how I must make my commitment, within this culture of belongingness to myself and to the things that identify and define me. Therefore, I have this increased sense of security.

"I don't think, with respect to the second question—about community—that I am in any contradiction if I move from the particular to the universal. I suspect those who love mankind but hate people. The one-world idea is beautiful, and I accept it; but I believe that it will be achieved only insofar as people are true to themselves at whatever level truth comes to them and reflects their cultures and their religious heritages. This in no way should be a source of divisiveness from other people."

One discussant, a Protestant clergyman, spoke of the small group that often forms in a church and serves as a shelter for its members in trouble. He noted that a kind of group therapy, sometimes unconscious and sometimes consciously guided, occurs in such a group. Another member remarked that some psychopathic hospitals had become integrated community structures, with everyone—the patients, the nurses, the orderlies, the attendants, the volunteers—exerting influence on the social system. This change had had gratifying results in the treatment of many disturbed people.

One of the Catholic priests recalled a remark made by a psychologist in the preceding session to the effect that back in the sixteenth century people had thought they knew everything about mental illness. In recent decades the main area of study had been disturbances occurring in one part of the personality structure—psychosexual development. Psychosocial and psychoreligious development have been neglected. It is known, however, that it was erroneous to think that if one cured the neurosis of a delinquent, that person would stop being a delinquent. It is necessary to cure a delinquent as such. The delinquent's social attitudes have to be changed.

Two discussants in this session, continued the priest, had said that therapists and religious advisers are often able to help the mentally disturbed person with their warmth and understanding. "I will agree that perhaps it may make this person's suffering much less, but I don't think it will effect a cure. When you have a problem in psychotherapy, which is a highly technical care, I think it has to be handled technically."

A psychologist disagreed with this latter view. "I wonder," he said, "if psychotherapy should be a technical procedure. I wonder if it ought not to be a nontechnical procedure, a completely lay procedure. As long as psychotherapy remains in the hands of any professional élite and is not translated into social movement, it is going to defeat its purpose. It seems to me that Rabbi Goldman touched on this when he said that psychiatry without a philosophy, without a commitment, without something to give the individual that he can take and make his own, is incomplete."

"I don't think these two points of view are antagonistic," said a physician. "I think that therapy is everybody's business, and everybody engages in it. Some of the best therapists I know are bartenders. But this doesn't mean that there is not a highly technical area in which expert knowledge is required to deal with the situation."

"I think," the priest added, "that the therapeutic relationship is a different thing from the highly technical procedures through which we resolve a psychological conflict. We must remember that a psychological conflict is something totally unconscious which is producing symptoms. Perhaps sometimes, I admit, we may help people in various ways, relieving them of various symptoms, without really curing them."

The implications of an individual's belonging to and withdrawing from a group were the subject of further discussion. It was agreed that this was an area calling for further study.

Bringing the group's attention back to the partnership of religion and psychotherapy, a psychiatrist told of a young patient of his whose early childhood rejections had led him to steal, along with other indications of disturbance. After several treatments that enabled the boy to conquer his guilt feelings to some degree, he was able to consult his minister, with highly successful results. The psychiatrist felt that religion—acceptance by his church—had accomplished more quickly what psychotherapy would have accomplished in time.

Another group member spoke briefly of the problems related to the religious-centered and -motivated person as not being necessarily mentally healthy. It is a question, he said, of ego organization at the adaptation level. Is it not possible, he asked, "that community-mindedness, the sense of community on one level and religion on the other, can provide an adaptation potential for a person who finds his particular organization of ego inadequate under stressful conditions?" If so, the speaker suggested, then if the society to which the person belonged, sick as it might be, were threatened with disintegration, he could adapt to a higher social organization, a larger milieu.

HORIZONS FOR THE FUTURE

CHAIRMAN
Frank Fremont-Smith, M.D.

HORIZONS FOR THE FUTURE

At the orientation session on Friday afternoon, three members of the symposium had been asked to serve as recorders, one for each of the three principal sessions. Their task was to outline, from the material discussed, directions in which future exploration might profitably be made by the Academy.

Chairman Fremont-Smith opened the final session by calling upon the recorders to present their suggestions.

Facing a program of "fantastic importance," Dr. Lauren H. Smith, one of the recorders, said one must define the services that can be rendered by the doctor, the religionist, and others concerned with mental health. Then, for effective coalescence of the functions of all these persons, improved communication is essential.

First priority for study Dr. Smith assigned to the roles of the various workers in psychotherapy, for theirs is the primary contact point: the rendering of service to those who need it. He believed that clinical studies and examples, made with simplicity and strongly based on experience, would be most effective.

Second, Dr. Smith suggested, should be a study in semantics. The sessions here had stressed the necessity for removing obstacles impeding communication among the many professions working toward the goal of improved mental health. Abstract as the problem may be, he considered it the key to further progress.

The third area of study he proposed was a survey of resources, of present practices, needs, and limitations at the clinical level, the community, parish, and household levels.

Dr. Loomis, another recorder, assigned first rating, out of the material developed at the second session, to the subject of values and health. He phrased it as a question: "What are the medical, psychological, sociological, and religious implications of the adaptations and maladaptations, especially regarding values, that allegedly lead to health or illness?"

Subsidiary questions Dr. Loomis suggested were: "What makes the difference in the values? Their source? Do they come through revelation of God? Or do they come through rational or empirical deduction? Is their apprehension by the individual simply a matter of saying, 'I believe in this'; or how is this belief expressed in life? This comes, I think, to a question posed in a previous session: 'What does religion really mean to people?' And then there is the tension between the values at aspiration level and actual achievement level, recognized and unrecognized in both cases."

The second area for study Dr. Loomis proposed was an investigation to find out whether the relation between religion and mental health lies in the subject matter itself, or in approaches to it, or in philosophizing about it. "Is man," he asked, "the central object, or subject, of concern for all of us working in the field? Or is the thing we have in common the caring function, our desire to help and understand our subject, the way we go about working with and in relation to man? Or is our common interest a philosophical approach to reality, a philosophical understanding of what we are undertaking?"

For his third proposition, Dr. Loomis raised the question whether religion is used by many workers in the mental health field as a technical instrument rather than as a positive good in its own right. "I feel that higher religion has to be related to and used not on the basis of 'where will it get me?' but for its own sake. We may discover that, as by-products, health, happiness, joy, common humanity, and a great many other things derive from it. But I feel that if we tackle it as an instrument or an aid and nothing but that, the very thing we think we are approaching will turn to ashes in our grasp."

A member of the group suggested that the point might be phrased: "Religion as end or means?" There was general approval.

The third recorder, Dr. Humphreys, had culled from the material presented at the third session as his first point for study the unitive functioning of the person in the integration of tissue function, particularly the role of anxiety in relation to the reactions of stress.

"If we focus upon the purely biological," he said, "then we are missing the boat. Attention to this matter involves the study of the democracy of the body, how the liver and the spleen and the heart all work together to establish a kind of democracy in which each organ plays its role, but in which each has its own unitive function with regard to the whole. This also involves the moral responsibility of the person toward the maintenance of homeostasis and his responsibility in the processes of maturation, and I believe that it helps to bring the priest and the pastor and the rabbi pretty close to the fields of biology." This is difficult, Dr. Humphreys admitted. It means trying to bring the ages together from a biological and cultural point of view.

Asked if the area could be called "unitive function of the individual at biological, sociological, emotional, and spiritual levels," Dr. Humphreys said this was correct, but warned that vertical as well as horizontal considerations should be included.

Dr. Humphreys' second proposed area for study was the interrelation between the phenomenal and the noumenal—the contributions of religion and the behavioral sciences, two sides of experience, to mental health. "I feel that this would bring us face to face with some of the most vital problems of our respective fields," he said. "Time and again religious literature has included reference to that which is a little bit beyond the phenomenal. Now, is there or is there not such a thing as the noumenal? This raises the possibilities of other aspects of reality." A participant asked whether Dr. Humphreys was using the word "noumenal" in the classic sense about the thing itself, or in the sense of the supernatural. Dr. Humphreys replied that he meant it in the sense of the metaphysical.

The third point Dr. Humphreys suggested was a study of the social function of religion. Much of the Saturday afternoon discussion had related to the subject of belonging, of alienation, "what Toynbee implies in his studies of the evolution of new bodies politic, our responsibility with reference to an evolving society. The study of belonging or of alienation of the individual and the group in either a democratic or a communistic society—the forces that bind us together are greater than the forces that tend to separate us—is a basic function of religion. Have we any responsibility in this direction?"

The chairman then asked the members of the group to suggest additional subjects for study.

A medical educator expressed concern with the question of educational growth versus indoctrination. "I think we all have in common a belief that the educational process is the way in which many of these problems are going to be worked out—perhaps through environment, perhaps through universities. I found myself increasingly uneasy last night at the frequent use of the word 'should.' I kept feeling that a great deal of what was spoken of as education was not really that, but indoctrination.

"How does one reach a predetermined goal? I thought of this overnight in terms of my own experience in medical education. Every profession represents a balance between education and training. Education is the growth of the individual. Training is the transference of knowledge and techniques and points of view and skill. I think it is important to understand that the medical-school people are working constantly to give the future physician a broad insight into man as a social being, to make him see that health and morality are largely superimposable concepts, and that social health and individual health involve a problem of morality.

"There is a different word to describe a community of effort. I think a study group ought to explore how one designs a real educational opportunity in which students come, not to achieve a predetermined end, but to grow in a true educational sense. One adds to the fruitfulness of the opportunity in which growth occurs with the points of view that are represented here.

"It is as important for us to understand the phenomenon of religion as it is to understand any of the other aspects of man. The thing we have in common here is an increasing understanding of man. We can provide a growth opportunity for an education in morals based on mobilizing all of man's concepts—his religious concept, his philosophical concept, his understanding of psychology, behavioral sciences, biochemistry, and theology."

A clergyman, speaking from his experience as a student and a teacher in seminaries, mentioned the inescapable question of "the willingness of the student to commit himself to the 'party line,'" as he called what the previous speaker had probably meant by indoctrination. He thought that a group such as the present one, looking at education with a broad perspective, could do much to help faculties, administrators, and boards of control to get a better image of themselves and of their purpose.

The fact that the conference had discussed religion without using the word "faith" seemed remarkable to one of the psychiatrists. He proposed a study of the synthesis of faith and scientific method, because this is the source of the clash between science and religion.

A Catholic priest found the word "indoctrination" troublesome. "After all," he said, "if you suggest that this should be translated into a seminary atmosphere, I think it must be realized that here we have a different framework. For instance, don't we both have something of the same problem? Isn't it the function of the medical school to impart a certain amount of information? If that is not done, you don't fulfill your function."

The medical educator replied that this depended upon the proper balance between education and training. The priest added: "What I object to is that it seems to me you suggest that the necessary effort to do this is not education, but indoctrination. These are getting to be labels. I think they are barriers to real communication."

The physician-teacher explained that to him the most important function of a medical school was to stimulate the student's curiosity, to enable him to recognize the existence of questions and to seek their answers, to see every patient as an experimental opportunity. He believed that in a seminary it would be important also to have "the greatest possible exercise of curiosity, speculation, exploration, growth in philosophical religious thinking and understanding of man—understanding of self as well as of others."

A special problem of the seminary, said a Protestant clergyman, is to train the student in the operation of his denomination, the religious bureaucracy, one might say. This kind of training may not give him the liberty to inquire about the nature of the organization. "The fine distinction between being able to ask why something is being done and at the same time to keep oneself a functioning member of the bureaucratic system is a very subtle kind of thing. If the prospective clergyman doesn't know what he is doing and at the same time know how he can ask questions in the right places, he is a lost soul as regards creativity in his job."

Turning to the third proposal made by Dr. Smith, a survey of practices at the community and clinical levels, a rabbi suggested that enough material had been accumulated to make it possible to look into what the psychiatrists and psychoanalysts as well as the religionists regard as the beneficial and detrimental aspects of religion in relation to human happiness.

"I think," he continued, "we might also find out what sources, let us say, a Catholic psychiatrist uses, or an atheistic psychiatrist, a Protestant psychiatrist, or a Jewish psychiatrist, who has brought his values into this system. I think we may find ourselves skating on thin ice here in problems of freedom and in other areas. It might be much more helpful and concrete if we could see each discipline acting in its own way within its own situation, and even what those without a religious viewpoint have done in these areas."

A psychiatrist proposed that a study group work on how the various religions approached mental health. "It seems to me that there is a kind of occupational hazard in this kind of conference. That we are looking for areas of agreement is good, of course; but if later on we try to communicate this to people outside, then this friendly, co-operative atmosphere may not always work. I am thinking particularly of the way we have been using the word 'religion' as if religion were one thing. What I suggest is that one of our study groups face concretely and directly this problem: what is common and what varies in the religious approaches to mental health?

"At a meeting under the auspices of the World Federation for

Mental Health not long ago, this question was asked: what does mental health look like to the Protestant, the Catholic, the Jew, the Buddhist, the Mohammedan, the Communist? What variations are there in the notions of what is mental health, depending upon the religious background?

"I would go much further than that. I would say: can you find something common in this particular area within the Protestant group, between, let us say, a rather strict Episcopalian and a Quaker or a Unitarian? In other words, what is there in terms of philosophy and of practice that would unite all religious groups in their attitude to mental health, and what must be taken into account as a separating factor?

"When we speak of religion and mental health, to what extent do we have to take into account the varieties of religion and religious experience? I might say that, since the Academy is a member association of the World Federation, there could be a very interesting co-operation and collaboration on this problem with the Scientific Committee of the Federation."

The speaker proposed a second area for study: the effect of various religious beliefs and practices on inter-group relations. "Religious identification is not quite the same as 'belonging.' It may possibly come under that, but it is a problem that was mentioned in an earlier meeting of the Advisory Committee of the Academy a year ago. We have talked about the possibility of conducting research in this field, and it still seems to me that the problem is important enough to be worth looking into with considerable care."

The chairman offered a suggestion about methods of studying such questions as were being raised here. He believed it more helpful to specify differences, variations, than to avoid them. Looking closely at the nature of a disagreement narrows the area of disagreement and releases larger areas of agreement. Arguments are not dangerous; there is no need to generalize about differences of opinion in a protective way. Reducing them to their real nature and then facing them squarely brings much better results.

Two more proposals were made by a Protestant clergyman. "I am assuming," he said, "that it is possible to be mentally healthy as a Catholic, as a Protestant, as a Jew, as an atheist, as a Buddhist, or as anything else. Is there any common denominator here? Could we draw a profile of the mentally healthy person broad enough to include a number of varieties but still definitive enough to give us some basic characteristics? I am thinking in particular of the problem of the tension between conformity and individuality. Is the organization man mentally healthy? Is the chronic rebel mentally healthy? And how about the degrees in between?"

For his second proposed study, he suggested a broad-based survey. "I have been somewhat surprised that with the exception of the rabbis present, there has been no parish priest or Protestant pastor in this gathering. From my own experience in the ministry, I know that, like it or not, trained for it or not, the parish minister or priest is on the firing line so far as mental health problems are concerned. They land in his lap, whether he knows how to deal with them or not, and often he has to proceed on the basis of what little knowledge he has, what common sense he may possess, and what knowledge of the community's resources he has been able to gather.

"Now, my suggestion is that there be research in the area of what ministers and priests actually do with these problems when they arise. Do they feel that they have the necessary training? Do they have relationships with psychiatrists? Do they know the community resources? What kinds of problem come to them? Do they know when to refer and when not to refer? All of these things, which I think could be embodied in a questionnaire that the Research Committee might work out, would give us a picture of what actually happens, not only in New York City, but in Sioux City, Iowa, or in any place in the country where there are just as many problems."

One of the recorders added two more proposals. "How are values and faiths unwittingly and nonverbally communicated from the preacher to his parishioners, from the doctor to his patient, from the psychiatrist to his patient, over and beyond the intentional and overt communication of putting them in words?"

The second suggestion had to do with the "communication to medical students of insights and knowledge about religion. There is a project in Chicago for putting a theologian on the medical-school faculty. This is a very important thing."

A psychologist remarked that he thought clergymen do not involve themselves sufficiently in psychology. Some of those present had said that they were not in any sense aspiring to train little psychologists or psychiatrists. "I think this somewhat apologetic attitude is a modest and in some ways proper one, but also somewhat unnecessarily limited. After all, there are many more clergymen in this country than there are psychologists or phychiatrists. The clergy are spread about the country; they are available to society in a way that psychologists and psychiatrists are not. Ministers have, so to speak, a shop that is used one day a week in general, and could be used six days a week. Churches in even the smallest village could be forces of psychotherapy and social revitalization in ways that they are not now being used. It seems to me that there is a potential here, physically and from the standpoint of personnel. It is also in line with great traditions and concepts. But the clergymen are still being very tentative and unself-confident about it."

A Protestant clergyman said that the preceding speaker had obviously assumed that the minister or priest is the person with both a commitment and a responsibility as far as religion is concerned, and he possibly had implied that the psychiatrist and others are secularizing the situation. "I suggest that some clergymen are secularists, and that some psychiatrists, sociologists, psychologists, have a religious commitment and some do not. It is essential that this be communicated, verbalized, within the context of the kind of responsibility we are envisioning here for the clergy. It will increase considerably the effectiveness of our role, our acceptability, in the institutions we may be related to in the general area of knowledge and practice."

"Working along with the doctors in a community," said a rabbi, "I find that what has been said is related to the whole question of authority from the viewpoint of the medical authority in the community and the pastor. It is not always clear where the boundary lines are. How far shall the pastor go in this therapy, and at what point can he induce danger? If he enters a counseling situation and is in trouble, can he possibly face the medical authorities? Usually we have some difficulties on this score. It seems to me that here is an area that ought to be clearly, or at least hopefully, defined. We are overwhelmed by the fact that we do not have the authority on a medical or health basis to deal with many problems."

EPILOGUE

EPILOGUE

The academic symposium reported in the preceding chapters, like the very founding of the Academy of Religion and Mental Health, marked a certain point in the changing relations between two once mutually suspicious groups—religious leaders and scientists. Only a generation ago, a meeting of this kind would have been impossible.

The rapprochement that has taken place between scientists and clergymen in recent years seems to be in large part the result of broadening outlooks on both sides. Scientists have expanded their range of interests to include entire areas of human behavior that were formerly considered outside the province of their study. Such things as values, personal issues, and even the self-involvement of the scientist have been accepted as worthy of and relevant to scientific interest. Although methodology in some of these areas is admittedly crude at present, one may confidently expect that adequate techniques will be developed precisely because these areas are now regarded as suitable for investigation.

The scientist has recognized lately that as a man he has concern for questions that even an expanding scientific field has not yet encompassed—notably religious and spiritual issues—but questions that are nonetheless inescapable realities in the total personality and in the world. In other words, the scientist no longer insists that everything can be studied or explained by scientific procedures now available, nor that what cannot be so studied or explained is unworthy of his notice.

Many theologians now look upon religious phenomena as appropriate subject matter for scientific inquiry, and do not feel that such inquiry is a threat to the reality. They recognize, also, that religious experience and practice are not an isolated segment of human behavior, but can be fully understood only as part of the total personality of the individual and of the community.

Emphasizing the inter-discipline approach to mental health that is the core of the Academy's efforts, the symposium brought together representatives of certain basic viewpoints of religion and science. Religion's spokesmen were clergy of three major faiths; science was represented by physicians and behavioral scientists.

One might object that the participants were too select a group, not fairly representing the large body of their colleagues. It is true that the scientists present were initially well disposed toward religion, as the religionists were sympathetic to scientific investigation; indeed, several of the latter were trained in branches of the behavioral sciences as well as in their theologies. A certain degree of sympathy, mutual respect, and recognition of common interests would be necessary if any basis for fruitful collaboration were to be laid. The members of this particular group, each a duly qualified specialist by the standards of his profession, gave clear indication, through participation in the two-day discussion, that they perceived the essential interdependence of their disciplines in the task of improving mental health. They may be regarded as forerunners in a movement that is gathering momentum.

In the conference sessions, as discussion leaders presented their views and threw out challenges, and as free exchange of opinion proceeded, the usual interaction among members of a group took place. It became clear that, well disposed to each other as clergy and scientist were, they approached the central problem of mental health from different points of view and expressed themselves in terms that were not always mutually intelligible. Semantic difficulties produced annoyance at many points. At times, it seemed they were a major block to communication. Again, members expressed concern lest preoccupation with communication be overemphasized, as if more precise agreement on definitions would magically dissipate all the differences between religionists and scientific workers in the mental health field. Vested interests, loyalties, divergent ways of thinking growing out of dissimilar training and experience, and personality differences, moved participants to react in different ways. Sometimes differences of opinion vanished under the melting influence of friendly discussion; again, they merely pointed out the need for more study of the subject. But beyond any possibility of doubt, communication of a most satisfying kind did take place, and a great measure of understanding and agreement was achieved.

The members of the symposium were keenly aware of the benefit they gained from the two days of fellowship with their colleagues, from the frank and free interchange of opinion, and the new insights into the thinking of associates in their professions and in others of different method and outlook but equal concern with human behavior. Despite the warmth of friendly understanding and the wide areas of agreement, however, there was unanimity of feeling that this conference, with its broadly phrased theme and the deep probing of its discussions, could be regarded only as an initiating event. The work begun here must be carried on by subsequent conferences devoting more intensive consideration to specific topics.

The major concern, therefore, of all members of the group, as the meeting neared its close, was the outlining of areas for future attention. The following aspects of mental health appeared to be among the most potentially rewarding subjects of further interdiscipline study:

Differentiation of roles among the various disciplines contributing to mental health.
Values as they affect the scientist and the clergyman in their theoretical and practical work.
Religion and the scientific method.
The individual and social function of religion in mental health.
Religion in the developing personality.*

---

* This subject was chosen as the title for the 1958 symposium.

The annual symposium, taking up these and related topics, is an important part of the Academy's program. Members of this symposium anticipated that study groups would be formed to deal with the problems suggested here more concretely and protractedly than could be done in an annual symposium. Sections of the Academy, groups of its associates, might also undertake part of the work. Informal contacts among individuals, notably among members of this conference, could contribute still more to the work begun here. These and many other forms of collaboration with universities, societies, and other institutions looking toward uniting the resources of religion and the medical and social sciences for man's benefit, are the steps the Academy hopes to take in the coming years. With the help of its members and friends, it moves confidently forward.

PARTICIPANTS

THE REV. GEORGE C. ANDERSON, New York, N. Y.
Director, The Academy of Religion and Mental Health

ANDRAS ANGYAL, M.D., Boston, Mass.
Formerly Director of Research, Worcester State Hospital,
Worcester, Mass.

KENNETH E. APPEL, M.D., Philadelphia, Pa.
Chairman, Department of Psychiatry, University of Pennsylvania; President, The Academy of Religion and Mental Health

GEORGE PACKER BERRY, M.D., Boston, Mass.
Dean, Harvard Medical School

THE REV. WILLIAM C. BIER, S.J., PH.D., New York, N. Y.
Chairman, Department of Psychology, Fordham University

GRAHAM B. BLAINE, New York, N. Y.
Partner, Tucker, Anthony, and R. L. Day; Trustee, The
Academy of Religion and Mental Health

GRAHAM B. BLAINE, JR., M.D., Cambridge, Mass.
Psychiatric Student Health Service, Harvard University

105